CW01522323

To//
MARIA

JOURNEY WELL

Jony

When Do The Tears Stop?

Joy Brisbane

authorHOUSE®

AuthorHouse™ UK Ltd.
500 Avebury Boulevard
Central Milton Keynes, MK9 2BE
www.authorhouse.co.uk
Phone: 08001974150

First published by AuthorHouse   9/21/2010

ISBN: 978-1-4520-6403-1 (sc)

First Published

Raider International Publishing U.S.A. 2008

This book is printed on acid-free paper.

Dedication

To Jeff... love cannot die!

આર્

Thank You

To Dallas Kinnear... with my heart-felt gratitude and love for the many hours you have given to this book, for the way you challenged me, for your encouragement, and for your faith in me. But mostly... thank you for your love.

Contents

Introduction

The grief of parting was not new to me, but there had been no grief to compare with the absolute loss I felt with the death of my soul-mate... my lover... my best friend... my husband, Jeff. At times the ravages of pain upon my mind and gut left me exhausted, tired of spirit.

All of a sudden, things that once felt important no longer mattered. Little things were what counted: Jeff's laughter across a room; only one toothbrush in the bathroom; the touch of his fingers on my back; cuddles in the early hours of morning and his lovely grey eyes suddenly welling up with warmth, tenderness and love.

It was the humanness of him, no longer accessible, that drove me to moments of utter loneliness, of gut-wrenching pain. The grief, frightening in its intensity, left me emotionally naked and raw. Doubts of long-held beliefs tugged at my mind, challenged my truth, my courage. Often the voices of friends and family sounded from a distance. And words of sympathy on cards, in letters, became blank pages.

But from deep within my heart a voice whispered. Almost against my rebelling will, the Spirit took its first tentative step on its new path of growth. My embarkation on a new life had begun. I was to learn that even in death there can be joy; that love cannot die; that communication with Jeff could still go on. He had simply shed his shell.

Out of my longing came an awareness of Jeff's presence. Like all who sense this for the first time, I wondered if it was my imagination. Being the strong energy he had always been, the persistent presentation of his love and presence in my life became too potent to simply excuse as the workings of the mind. Time after time he validated his on-going existence. I began to comprehend that, in the disembodiment of the soul, the binding negative elements disintegrate and we become pure love, pure light.

I have learned to communicate with Jeff, to open my heart once more to his love. I have also learned to let go of him and to walk my own path. I have become more deeply aware that life before and beyond the grave is a wondrous journey.

Within these pages are my tears and laughter. It is my dearest wish that, in sharing this journey, the love and help I received will be imparted to those who know the devastating pain of grief. If you gain one small gem of wisdom or help from this book then it will have all been worthwhile.

Joy

Chapter One - The Parting

At seven in the morning, on the seventeenth of January two thousand and two, my husband Jeff rose from our bed. His strong, sensual back sent waves of pleasure to my throat. At seventy seven, his body held the beauty of years of hard work that had kept it fit and youthful. We had been together for over twenty-four years, and still he could ignite the fire of passion within me.

I could clearly visualise the moment we first met. The smouldering look in his grey eyes reached inside me and brought to life a sensuality that had remained dormant through a previous marriage. He had found the key to unlock the door to my womanhood. A womanhood I had long kept safely guarded, imprisoned deep within me. I remember looking into his magnificent grey eyes and thinking, "I'm in trouble."

On that morning of January the seventeenth he turned to face me as he dressed. "Stay where you are, Darling. I have to fix the pump on the dam. It won't take long. Then I'll come back and get you breakfast in bed."

We had friends, Trisha and John, from England staying with us. He had planned to fix the pump early so we could spend the rest of the day in their company.

As Jeff pulled on his shirt a voice within me said, "Go with him." I stretched, pulled back the covers and said, "I'm coming with you." Love, as it so often did, welled up in his face as he replied, "That's lovely, but I won't be long. You might as well enjoy these moments alone." My voice within cancelled the sleepy desire to remain between the sheets. "No, I'm coming with you." How thankful I am that I heeded that voice!

The morning was crisp and clear. The summer's heat had not yet singed the air. The dam was five hundred metres away, snuggled in a valley in a dry eucalypt forest in the south eastern part of Australia. We held hands as we walked, enjoying the songs of our much-loved birds while smelling the perfume of the trees and looking for orchids.

I sat on the bank of the dam watching my man at work. A breeze sent ripples scudding across the surface of the water, distorting the mirror images of trees. I threw pebbles adding ripples to ripples. How lucky I was to be a part of this land, sharing it with my mate. It was such a poignant moment of peace and love, flowing within and around me.

Jeff completed his task, gathered up his tools and walked towards me. I rose to give him a hug. As he came close, a grey shadow spread across his sun-tanned face. I looked into his eyes and fear gripped my heart with steely coldness.

"Are you all right?" I asked. He stagged a little and replied, "No. Actually I don't feel all that good."

They were the last words he spoke.

He lay down on the bank of the dam. His eyes, now full of deep emotional pain, longing and love, looked into my face, conveying the knowledge that he was dying. Not with words did we say goodbye, but with a welling up of all the deep love and passion we had shared since the first moment we met. In that moment came the greatest pain I have ever known; a pain that pierced every cell of my being and exploded in screams.

I felt split in two. My human self, absorbed in the trauma of knowing Jeff was dying. My soul, standing back, watching the scene, was noting all that was happening.

My human self, began to scream. Jeff's eyes rolled upwards until only a portion of his pupils could be seen, as though he was watching his own soul leave. Panic froze my mind. In desperation I began heart massage and applied mouth-to-mouth resuscitation trying to bring him back. Yet all the time I was working on his body I knew it was useless. The trained nurse within me said, "It's over," but the lover screamed over and over, "No! Not yet! No!"

Eventually I let go. His time to leave Earth had come. The immediate pain of his death was crippling. I knelt beside his still body, disbelief surging through me, a great chasm of blackness inside. In the stillness of the forest, I hugged him one last time. Torrents of tears flowed onto his lifeless chest. A part of me had died with him.

Farewell

One last look,
as you lay on the ground,
one last moment of love and
in your grey eyes such deep sorrow.
My voice, harsh, ragged,
slashed a trail through the trees.
You knew you were leaving.
Your last breath trickled over your lips.
Silent forest! The only sound
my frantic heartbeat
thumping in my ears.
Even my scream seemed distant.
I will always remember
that last look, the deep sorrow,
the upward turn of your eyes
and, then, the blank, lifeless stare.

My soul watched his soul leave his body. Like a shadowed form of his human self, it slid from his feet up and out through the top of his head as a hand would slide from a glove, or feet sliding out from long-legged boots. Faintly visible, it was a field of bluish energy moving out and up into the air.

As I look back on that day, the two halves… my human self and my soul… stand quite separate, but equally strong, in my memory. Perhaps, ironically, it was for me the first true realisation and understanding of how a soul is a separate entity from its human form.

One of my most precious memories occurred within the last minute of Jeff's life.

Since the age of seven, I have been aware of an ability to 'tune in' to dead people and talk to them. As a child I had one person in particular I used to play tennis with. I would hit the ball up against my father's wooden garage door and my friend in spirit would chat to me as I did so. Sometimes I saw her against the garage door as though she was playing with me. I learnt quickly not to speak of those I saw in spirit as my parents believed I was not telling the truth when I said I could see my friends. Later I came to realise such a person was called a medium. Even though I never spoke of it again to my parents, I was one of the luckier children who did not close down this precious gift but silently carried the knowledge of it for many years. Jeff could not accept this part of me either. After a last attempt to get him to understand that this was a very real part of my existence, an attempt that ended in my being told I was fantasising and I needed to get rid of such ridicules notions, I once again went into silence.

In that last minute of Jeff's life he knew the truth of what I had been telling him. He 'saw' his beautiful guardian angel waiting to help him cross over. A massive strong beam of white light poured down over him, but not only did it pour over him, it also poured through me to him…..the fullness and completeness of love in all of its power and compassion. In that moment he knew and I knew this was goodbye.

With it came a knowing of great joy and freedom, as though he were yelling, "Yes! I am out of here. I am free!" The stillness of the forest was complete. Not a bird sang. The breeze had stilled and the water became a perfect mirror of the trees. There was total eerie silence, breathless stillness, a pervading feeling of reverence. It was as though the forest was cradling his newly released soul in its gentle and loving energy. There was in that moment a sense of the divine.

For weeks to come, the dam and surrounding forest held in its energy an amazing stillness and reverence. It was so noticeable that other people, who knew nothing of how or where Jeff had died, would comment on the difference between that area and the rest of the forest. I often tested this phenomenon by taking visitors for a walk and without telling them why, would walk to the dam. As we approached the dam we seemed to step through an invisible curtain into a huge dome of silence. No one who walked there remained untouched by the experience. It was like stepping onto sacred ground.

All his working life, Jeff had been a forest officer in the alpine areas of Victoria's Great Dividing Range, or in the drier forests of its central highlands. He had always said, "When I die I want to return to the forest."

And he did.

Chapter Two - The First Week

Jacob's Star

See that star,
the one on its own,
the big one
past the small bunch?
Can you see it?
That's my Grandfather!
I know it is
'cause I felt him there.
And anyway
he was bright
just like that star.
A light in the darkness!

As a grief counsellor, I have become aware, whilst helping people on their journey through grief, that at some stage many have encountered the presence of their loved one. Through a direct visitation or through signs that are undeniably connected to the one who died. Most people are hesitant to tell others of what they have seen or heard. They fear two things. Firstly, they fear that this special experience was 'only their imagination,' and that they may have a mental problem, even though the encounter was a powerful one. Secondly, they fear the response from well-meaning friends and family… that it was only wishful thinking and that such things don't happen. Thus they remain silent, not realising that this is, in fact, a common experience.

In life, Jeff was a powerful spirit. He either drew people to him, magnetized by his charisma and strength, or he repelled them because they could not deal with his blatant ownership of this sense of power. In spirit, his strength and power continued to come through. Jeff methodically went to each member of the family, and some of our close friends, letting them know he was still with them.

The signs were too many and detailed to recount them all. I would like to share a few of the more extraordinary.

For me, he chose the two aspects of nature for which I knew he had a special feeling… his favourite birds, the galahs and his favourite animals, the wallabies and kangaroos. He knew that, in choosing them, I would instantly recognise his connection to what was happening.

To the south of our few acres of land, set in a valley, a large flock of galahs, beautiful pink and grey birds of the parrot family, had a selection of white gum trees that was their home base. Many of those trees had hollow branches ideal for nesting. Each morning, the galahs would fly north over the valley and our home, heading for open fields where they would spend the day feeding. Jeff would call out to them and they would chatter and screech in reply. They were masters of flight, those galahs, diving, banking, swooping between the trees in playful fashion, finally to rise above the tops of the gums and disappear out of sight. It became a daily ritual between Jeff and the birds. At eventide, they would return to their nests.

The morning after he died, at eight forty-five, exactly twenty-four hours after he had left his body… I could hear the galahs coming down the valley before I could see them. As I looked to the south they came towards me, a large flock in the formation of a V. I had never seen such a formation with these birds before. The only sound was of their wings, an eerie, loud whooshing. Not a single screech or chatter. With purposeful flight, they moved low through the valley, rose up and over our home, dipping down again before rising over the tree tops and out of sight.

Through it all they kept their V formation and remained silent. The eeriness of that moment sent tingles all over my skin and chills up and down my spine. I had no doubts. They were acknowledging Jeff's spirit in their midst. I felt as though a knife had been thrust deep into my chest. Never again would he stand here calling to his galahs as they flew, playfully, over his head, watching their flight.

The second sign Jeff sent to me came through his favourite wallaby. For the eighteen years we had lived with this land surrounded on three sides by state forest, he had developed a special and unique communication with the kangaroos and wallabies. On several occasions, we had old and dying wallabies come to our home to see their last days through. Somehow they knew that our land was a safe haven. Jeff was able to hand feed these wild creatures, often with offerings from his vegetable garden. I have a vivid memory of him cupping water in his hands and holding them to a wallaby's mouth, allowing it to drink during its last hours of life. And then I shared his tears as we laid the wallaby in its final resting place.

There was one female wallaby to which he had a particular attachment. She came to understand that if she were at his vegetable garden at a certain time of evening, then it was highly likely she would obtain some crisp lettuce leaves or the tops of carrots. This wallaby appeared shortly after Jeff died, in the middle of that day. Regardless of the movement of ambulance drivers, police, the coming and going of friends and family, she never left until after his funeral some five days later. During that time, she remained close to his vegetable garden or close to the front of our home. The evening of his funeral, she left and I never saw her again.

Jeff's funeral was held in an area of bush close to our home. This particular area he used to call his art gallery. It was a reef of rock that ran for about five hundred metres on a slight hill. The centuries had covered these rocks with moss, ferns, and wild orchids. Between the rocks grew a variety of trees. According to his wishes, it was there we scattered his ashes.

Jeff's directive was to spread his ashes over the ground and rocks, to cast them to the wind. The problem was there was no wind. It was a still summer's day. I had my back to my family and friends who stood further down the hill. My head was down as I concentrated on my task. When the urn was empty, I stood up and turned towards them. There was a look of amazement and awe on their faces.

Later my daughter said, "Mum, you didn't see what happened, did you?" There were areas where the ashes had piled up. A sudden gust of wind… the only one for the entire day… had lifted the ashes up into the foliage of the smaller trees, casting the white ash over the face of the hill, spreading it on rocks, earth, fallen leaves and grass. There was a knowingness among those gathered there that Jeff was making sure his wishes were fulfilled.

After the ceremony, we all made our way back to the house for refreshments; all except Jeff's youngest son who remained behind, needing time to be alone in his grief. Suddenly he found himself in the midst of hundreds of butterflies. From whence had they all come? He took photos of them. After processing, not a single butterfly was to be seen in those photos.

Being a man who lived close to nature, Jeff, after his death, used nature to bring awareness of his presence to those he loved. There were, however, other ways he made his presence known.

A friend, who lived in Hawaii, had been playing her CD's one evening. On retiring, she had left a CD in the player. She had turned the player off, including the switch at the wall. During the night her CD began to play. When she went to see what was going on she found her player was still turned off, including at the wall. On another occasion a friend woke during the night to the sound of her music box playing. When she switched on her light, she saw that the lid of her music box was still closed, yet the music continued to play. Yet another friend awoke from a deep sleep to the sensation of someone holding her hand. She knew it was Jeff.

This sense of physical touch was something I was to experience many times through the months to come.

The only person he actually appeared to in spirit form was my son. Again it was night time. During the third night after Jeff died, my son woke with the sense that someone was in his bedroom. He saw Jeff standing by the door. In a few seconds he conveyed to my son that all was well and not to be concerned, and then he faded from view.

According to some who have studied the journey of souls, it is unusual for a newly departed soul to appear, or bring signs of their presence through to loved ones, so soon after departing from their bodies. It is thought that souls need a period of time to rest, reunite with their soul family, and get used to being back in spirit form. It is testimony to Jeff's strength and powerful energy, so evident during his life, that he was able to come to us almost immediately after his death.

Chapter Three - Humour

(The names of the people at the funeral parlour have been changed to safeguard their identity)

Sorry

I know you would disapprove.
Me sitting here
grabbing tissues out of a box,
wiping my eyes, my nose with trees.
The problem is
I have run out of handkerchiefs.
"Well, wash them," I hear you say.
But I don't want to move.
I want to sit here,
let the tears release the pain,
let this big knot unravel.
Sorry! I need another tissue.

I found humour to be an essential part of dealing with my grief. Remembering the funny things that happened during my loved one's life, sharing those memories, were life jackets that helped to keep my head above water. Humour kept me from drowning in my ocean of sorrow.

There is no need to feel guilty when you find yourself laughing. Laughter in the early stages of dealing with grief was, for me, the beginning of the healing process. It was as vital as drinking water. There are tears enough in grief. Humour sits on the other side of the scale and helps us to keep our balance.

Such humour began the very next day after Jeff had gone.

On the day of Jeff's death, the funeral director sent a man out in the early afternoon to collect his body. We lived at the end of a dirt track deep in the forest. Our block of land was quite isolated. The driver arrived in a battered old van. He was wearing jeans and a checked shirt. At first I did not realise he was from the undertaker. When he opened the back doors I could see the inside of the van was tastefully furnished. A great deal of thought had been given to transporting a body with sensitivity and reverence. When I questioned the driver as to why he used a battered-looking van, he replied, "Do you want everyone to know I am driving your husband to the undertaker? This way people think I am just going for a bit of a drive through the bush… probably with a chainsaw in the back. No one would suspect I have your husband on board. Believe me, under the bonnet, this van is as good as new. I will get him safely back to town." Jeff would have enjoyed that exit, bumping along our dirt track in a battered old van.

The next morning, Tania, my daughter, and I headed into town to begin funeral arrangements. The day had a surreal quality to it. Nothing seemed real, least of all the idea of having to arrange for Jeff's farewell. John, our English friend, drove us into town. The glow of sunlight, filtering through the trees, seemed out of place. Why did the birds have to be so vibrant with their colours and songs? My pain-filled heart was affronted by such beauty.

After knocking for some time on the parlour door, we heard shuffling sounds and the noise of a key turning in the lock. I envisaged large old keys dangling from some ancient monk's gown, and half expected the door to creak with the effort of opening. Tania and I looked at each other quizzically.

Before us stood a very tall but quite stooped man, one shoulder much lower than the other, who walked with an accentuated limp. He said nothing until I explained who I was and that I had an appointment with Cindy. "Cindy's running late," he replied.

"You'd better come in and I'll get Jo to make you a cup of tea." He then lurched into the inner labyrinth of the parlour and disappeared from view. We stepped inside and waited.

Jo was a giant of a woman. Dressed in white shirt and black trousers, she was as tall as the man would have been if he had straightened up. Where he was thinly built, Jo had the arms and shoulders of a footballer, broad and all muscle. Her shoulders and chest came down to a V at her waist. She spoke in a deep, booming voice. Neither she, nor the man, helped to dispel my feeling that the world had taken on a surreal quality. As she marched away to get us coffee, my daughter looked at me and asked, "Well, I wonder what she does for a living then?"

We began to laugh as the image of this woman lifting coffins by herself flashed into our minds. We meant no disrespect towards Jo. We realised it was a form of release to see the funny side of it all.

Thankfully, Cindy was a very compassionate woman, for the mood had been set and, amidst the tears, Tania and I laughed spontaneously throughout the interview. Bless her! Cindy knew it was a way of releasing the tension and trauma we were feeling with the task of preparing for our loved one's farewell.

Chapter Four – The Last Rite

Bush Burial

Not the deep tearing of earth,
the wretched lowering down
of highly polished wood.
Not the standing on the edge
of grief's dark hole
to farewell lifeless flesh.
Rather... spread my ashes
where earth and moss welcome me
and orchids bloom eternally.
Dust to dust – yes,
but the spirit flies free
on its wondrous cosmic journey.
Sing no mournful strains
of soulful anguish for the dead.
Let the lusty chorus of birds
pervade the forest with their songs,
and let the kookaburra laugh
as charcoal shadows grow black and long.
From the seed of life I began, to the seed of life
I return that I may be born again.
When spring flaunts her pretty dress
see how the orchids,
once dead from Summer's heat,

rise green again and bloom anew.
Not the deep tearing of earth,
the wretched lowering down
of highly polished wood.
Spread my ashes
where stones and grasses welcome me
and orchids bloom eternally.

The day before Jeff's funeral I went into town to collect his ashes… now securely placed inside a pottery urn. The urn had straight sides and was wide at the top. Gracing its lovely glazed exterior was a design of trees. On arriving home I created a simple altar on Jeff's writing desk; a piece of lace cloth on which I sat the urn, candles and Jeff's photo.

The family had gathered and we were walking down memory lane together. Each one throughout the evening owned their grief with tears. I told them where Jeff's ashes were. Anyone wishing to spend time alone with their feelings of grief could do so in the quietude of that room. Jacob, the youngest of the grandchildren, aged six years, visited the altar with his mother. When they returned she had a smile dancing in her eyes.

"He wanted to look in the urn", she whispered. "He thought Jeff had shrunk and was curled up inside."

I realized that Jeff's death must seem very strange to my young grandson, and that, in dealing with my own grief, I must not forget his bewilderment and pain. I decided the best way to help him was in being honest with him. So I answered his questions gently and truthfully. I feel small children know when they are not being told the truth and it only adds to their confusion and grief.

Knowing what was ahead the following day, I could not sleep. Black elastic stretched the hours. I watched and waited for night to let go of the darkness. The morning twanged back upon me and the pain of loss numbed my mind.

Stony Clay

The moon meets the dawn,
and the long hours of night
find closure with grey light.
I sit at the water's edge that laps,
with whispers, the stony clay,
gazing at the ground
where you lay down
to take your last breath.
There is no sign now,
no flattened grass, no kicked stones.
Only the memory remains of that final breath,
and the pained look of farewell in your eyes.
My love, I could not sleep.
The bed became a burden.
So I have come here, walking
in moonlight to be with you.
I need you, my Darling, today I need you.
Our family and friends gather
to scatter your ashes, to remember, and
for this day alone, to cry as one.
My tears reach far beyond
the stars that now disappear.
Grey light gathers around my grey heart.
Never again will our love-play be soaked in moonlight.

Yet, even on the day of his funeral, humour once again arose to balance the scale.

My son was escorting me to the place where we were to scatter Jeff's ashes. After we had walked about sixty metres along the forest track, Robert said, "Mum has someone else got the urn?" Oh my god! Can you believe it? Here I am off to my husband's funeral and where are the ashes? Still back at the altar! As Robert turned to get them Jeff's oldest son, called, "Joy, you didn't forget the old man did you? I thought this is what today was about."

I had this image of Jeff laughing, shaking his head and saying, "That's my woman, that's my Joy!"

Chapter Five - Alone

No matter how prepared we may be for the death of a loved one in our minds, we can never prepare the heart for the shock, the flood of emotions when that final breath is taken and released. Even though death may be a sweet release for those who have suffered, for the ones left behind the pain of loss in that moment of departure is no less for that knowledge.

The love and comfort of family and friends are priceless gifts to be treasured. For those who do not have this support, the journey of grief is a lonely one indeed.

My friends and family quickly gathered on that fateful day to support me and do what they could to help. Trisha and John, our visitors from England, became quiet and solid workers in the background. They, too, were in shock and yet they worked on without thought for themselves. I have no idea how many sandwiches and cups of coffee or tea Trisha made. Nor, in the haze of all that was happening, did I fully know what John did to keep my home running smoothly. My daughter made countless phone calls – perhaps the hardest task of all. People came and left, each one contributing in their own lovely way.

My Lovely One

Through the pain of death
you gently held me.
You, child, became my mother.
Tell me, in helping me to grieve,
when did you grieve, my Daughter?
Whilst I recalled the memories,
spoke of times gone by
with my departed lover,
held those pictures to my heart,
when did you speak, my Daughter?
Whilst the tears tumbled
through the sleepless nights:
whilst friends caringly held me,
who held you, my lovely one?
When did you cry, my Daughter?

There comes a time when the rituals of farewell have been performed and family and friends, rightly, return to their own lives. One is finally alone. Only then do we fully understand how this loss is going to impact on our lives.

After Jeff's funeral, after the sleepless nights and blur of days filled with people and things to be done, my mind and body were so exhausted I blissfully fell into a deep and dreamless sleep.

As I woke early the following day the surreal haze had disappeared. I looked across to the empty side of our bed. In that moment came the full realization that I was now completely alone. Never again would his head rest upon that pillow; nor would his lovely grey eyes, in their dreamy way, look across into my brown eyes.

Never again would I hear him say, "Good morning, Beautiful! I love you!" Never again would he wrap his arms around me, my head on his chest, and quietly talk about things that mattered to him. Never again would I be given that first cup of coffee followed by breakfast in bed.

Sunrise

"Are the nights difficult?" she asked.
"When do you miss him the most?"
It's a brilliant sunrise, my Love.
How I remember
snuggling in to you
as dawn spread
its soft pearl-grey light.
Your hand, with its crooked finger,
sleepily massaging my head
whilst the rising sun
flushed drifting clouds
with its vibrant personality.
That first kiss on the forehead,
conveying contentment and peace,
will linger always.
I watch the deep red evaporate.
How I cherished those moments,
rising from the dream world of Morpheus
to feel your arms
protectively encircle me.
I miss those early morning talks.
I miss the sound of your voice
penetrating my thoughts
as they clumsily surfaced
from their night's meanders.
The red has gone.
The grey of day is cold.
Frost clutches the earth in its relentless grip.
And your side of the bed is empty!

The full weight of responsibility was like an iron ball in the pit of my stomach. I became aware of all the tasks Jeff used to do, things as partners we tend to take for granted. The solar system batteries had to be cared for and the pumps and generators serviced. Water had to be pumped from dams. Wood had to be gathered, sawed and chopped. Cars had to be serviced. During the hot summer period, fire-fighting equipment had to be constantly tested, and procedures to reduce the risk of wild fire had to be completed. So the list went on.

I felt very much alone. I regretted having taken for granted all the seemingly ordinary events we shared each day. Little things became difficult or far more meaningful than those things I once felt were important. Little things, such as only one toothbrush in the bathroom, would bring tears streaming down my cheeks. The smell of Jeff in clothes that I had to give away brought sharp pains to my chest. For a long time I could not sit at the table alone to have my meals. The memory of his laughter across a room; the touch of his hand on my back; the quick little words we would say to each other that no one else understood; it was these simple little things that tore at my heart with gut-wrenching pain. Now that Jeff was gone, I suddenly realised how important the little things are that we share with our partners.

To cope with this sense of aloneness, and the fear of knowing I was alone, I became disciplined in meditating daily. I did not allow the discipline to become a chore and, therefore, rob me of the pleasure of being in that space. The how, where or when of going into meditation was not important. The only thing that mattered was doing it on a daily basis. There are no rules with meditation, no such thing as a right or wrong way to meditate. People who jog each day can be in a state of meditation. The same can be said of long distance bike riders, or those who go for long walks by the sea or in forests. To sit in silence and listen to the sounds of nature is a form of meditation. Gardeners are often in a state of meditation as they lovingly work with Mother Earth. Becoming absorbed in a beautiful piece of music is another way to meditate.

There are several ways that work for me. Perhaps the one I use the most is to clear my mind of all chatter; to totally relax my body to the point of no longer being aware of it; to go inwards and find the deep, still, peaceful place that is my true self, the spirit or the soul of me. Mostly I use music to move into this tranquillity. (See chapter 9).

I realized that the more I practised going into that place of quietude, the quicker it happened and the deeper it became. It was in this state of simply *being* I found the courage and strength to cope with the pain of loss and deal with all the challenges of this new life into which I had been abruptly thrust. In this place of *being* came the peace, the rest which my mind and soul craved from the ravages of negative emotions. In this state of stillness came the answers to questions, the lessening of confusion. I felt at one with the universal energy, that wondrous cosmic life-force, and was wrapped in a flow of warmth, love and compassion.

Chapter Six - Faith

Our faith is tested when we are left to deal with the rigours of death and life alone. We need faith in our ability to cope, to move forward, pushing our way through the grey cloud of confusion that threatens to swallow our vulnerable self.

Not only was my faith in myself vigorously tested, but so were my spiritual beliefs. Long held convictions at times became fragile lace tossing in wild stormy winds. I had always believed that the body was just a shell, a vehicle in which the soul resided until death separated the soul from that shell. After my mother's death, she had often communicated with me. I believed strongly in the on-going existence of the soul, and the ability to reincarnate. Now doubts and confusion stabbed my mind as fear played its part. What if my beliefs were wrong, and my experiences a figment of my imagination?

Slowly, and with a lot of persistence on Jeff's behalf, I began to trust what I was hearing and feeling. Yes, feeling! I would feel his hands touching my shoulders or his hand in my hand. First thing in the morning, I would feel him run his fingers through my hair, as he had always done before we rose from our bed. Whilst other signs have faded, as I have grown stronger, I still feel this sign of his presence.

On a daily basis he validated his presence. In the early stages of my grief, that validation was a blessing, a comfort, and yet at the same time a piercing pain in my heart, for it was a constant reminder that he was not here in the flesh. It was truly agony and ecstasy entwined in a cord of emotions.

On a practical level he also showed his presence. Synchronicity was a word to which I had given little thought. Yet, as days moved into weeks and then into months, I became aware through a constant series of events, that I was being helped in a way I had not recognized before. That help had been given to me all through my life, but it was not until my need became greater that I started to see it. Months have now turned into years and still the help continues.

The more I acknowledged Jeff's presence, the stronger grew our connection and the more help I gained. It was, and remains, my greatest lesson in trust, my deepest lesson in faith. With that trust, a beautiful calmness and peace grew within me. With the deepening of my faith came an awareness of the presence of other unseen beings, from the cosmic realm, helping me.

There are two events that remain in my memory as clear as the day they occurred. Both took place within the first few weeks after Jeff's death.

We lived in an isolated little valley. To get to our home one had to negotiate eight kilometres of rocky, pot-holed and, in places, eroded dirt track. Ours was not an easy home to call into for a cup of tea.

The cost of bringing regular power to the property, through rocky, forested land was prohibitive, so our home was run on solar energy. Choosing to live in this beautiful place also meant choosing a lifestyle of dependence upon our own generated power. The responsibility of keeping this system running smoothly now became mine.

A new type of solar light globe had just come on the market, using far less energy. I decided to make the change as these globes would help to conserve energy throughout the darker winter months. They were easy to install, except for one light that hung over the dining table. This light had a reflective white shade to spread the glow over the table. To change this globe also required changing the socket. I did not realise, as I began the task, that I needed four hands, two to hold the shade and two to install the socket.

After two hours of extreme frustration and copious tears, I threw the tools onto the table and screamed, "Why did you have to die? This is your job, not mine. If you want me to do this bloody job then please send me some help."

Thankfully I had been sensible and put an old blanket on our lovely polished table or it would have been damaged by the force with which I threw those tools. In that moment of pain in my grief, I actually hadn't realised the foolishness of my outburst. Jeff had not asked me to change to new light globes….it was all my own doing.

Ten minutes later there was a knock on the door. Our lovely friend, Narelle, looked at my tear-stained face and said, "I had this sudden feeling, an urge that I should come and see you. I felt you needed help."

Twenty minutes later the job was completed. Jeff, knowing me as well as he did, probably knew I would finally throw a tantrum when I realised I could not finish the task alone. It was a lesson in learning to let go of my stubborn determination and to ask for help.

All too often I have struggled alone, not wanting to be a burden to friends and family. I was to learn help comes in many forms. Not necessarily in the way we want or expect it to, yet come it will if we can let go our pride and ask. When I look back over the past years I can see the extent to which that help was given. Often it came in quiet and subtle ways, hidden within the routine of my daily life. Gradually, I learned to see the signs of that help, and to understand and acknowledge the love, compassion and support of my beloved and others.

The second validation of support came in a rather dramatic way. I can still feel tingling sensations through my body when I recall that day.

Whenever we had thunderstorms I had to disconnect our telephone and computer. If I didn't the micro chips were damaged and rendered both useless. Past experiences had been expensive lessons. Living on my own in isolation, I could not afford to be without my telephone.

Whilst shopping forty minutes away from where I lived, I happened to glance to the south. A huge volume of black threatening cloud was moving at a fast pace over my home. I knew there had to be strong winds behind it and the possibility of lightning strikes. It had been a beautiful late autumn day when I left with no sign of such weather approaching. I had left both the telephone and the computer connected.

I threw my shopping into the car and headed for home. Twenty minutes later, as I was about to enter the forest, lightning began to fork from cloud to land. One particular strike I knew was close to where I lived. Into the roar of the thunder I yelled, "No. Don't let there be any damage. Please look after my home. Don't let the phone and computer blow." Wind was bending the trees sending debris flying. I feared for my safety as I entered the forest. "Please, oh God, please help me. Get me home safely. Look after my home and all within it."

To my absolute amazement, across the road, under the canopy of trees, a rainbow appeared. With what information I had retained from my schooling, I knew this was almost impossible. The blanket of black cloud had reduced the light considerably.

The air was heavy and dark. It had begun to rain but there were no rays of sunshine. Then the heavens opened. A deluge of rain sheeted down. I had to stop driving as I could not see beyond the bonnet of the car. The combined roar of thunder, rain and wind was deafening and terrifying. Frozen with fear I screamed, "Help me! For God's sake help me!"

The rain eased. The wind dropped. Thunder still roared as the sky displayed its fireworks. Spread out before me was a huge sheet of water. I knew it would not be the only sheet of water I would have to drive through. Others would be deeper. Beneath that water were rocks and clay. The possibility of damage to my car and being stranded without communication, were real. Again I cried out, "Please! Please help me!" Tears streamed down my face. I looked up and there, just a short distance in front of me, another rainbow appeared, again under the canopy of the trees and across the road. Once might be a fluke of nature. Twice, it was a miracle and a sign that I was being cared for. I dried my tears. I knew it was going to be all right. With that second rainbow came calmness within me. I gave thanks to whoever was watching over me, and spent the next forty-five minutes negotiating the flooded track into my home.

As I arrived home the clouds parted and the sun sent golden ribbons of light through the trees. The ground was carpeted with leaves and small branches but no damage had occurred. The telephone and computer were still working. I made a cup of coffee and sat on the veranda. What was normally just a gentle stream eighty metres in front of the house, quickly became a roaring, raging river carting rocks and broken limbs of trees in its billowing brown water.

Tears of gratitude flowed. I knew I was being cared for and watched over. I knew I had just witnessed a miracle. My heart and mind were filled with awe and joy. A profound love welled up within me for Jeff, for the unseen hands that held me in their care, and for the wonderful gift of life. I had survived, my home had survived and I knew I was not alone.

Fog

In this silence
you are here,
so very close,
and yet…
Like this fog,
this eerie silence,
you are untouchable!

Chapter Seven - Guides

Since my early twenties I have been aware of an unseen presence beside me. For a number of years I paid little attention to that being's constancy in my life. As my children grew and I moved out of my first marriage into another, I slowly became more aware of the influence this being was having upon me. Like a flower opening gently to the sun, I understood and began to accept that I had certain psychic powers.

I believe we are all born with psychic abilities. Every precious new-born baby is highly in tune with its psychic self. Parents are now beginning to realise that when their little ones talk about their invisible playmates it may not be 'just their imagination.' When we enter into the stream of life, and go to school, we start to forget our spirit playmates, our guides, for it becomes no longer acceptable to speak of them. Reluctantly, and with the pain of growing into adulthood, most of us leave behind what we have been told is a world of fantasy. However, I am discovering such so-called fantasies are as real, if not more so, than this Earth-life we are living.

I knew that somehow this presence had something to do with awakening to my spiritual and psychic self. Through meditation, I began to communicate with this being. Eventually he revealed himself to me. One day, within the quietude of my meditation, a most beautiful man stood before me. Radiant white light surrounded him and seemed to come from within him. I asked who he was. He replied, "Call me Master!" For a long time I tried to get him to tell me his name. He always replied, "Why is a name so important to you? I have told you to call me Master."

I have long since stopped trying to find out who my Master is. It is enough to experience his wisdom, compassion and love. There is a sense that he has been with me through many lifetimes. As our connection grew, so did my love for him. Through these years of learning to stand alone, through my deepest, blackest time of grief, my Master gently held me in his light of love. My heart is filled with gratitude. I am in awe of this beautiful being.

Master

Master of the higher realms,
the power of love, and compassion
radiate from your beautiful being.
I am your student of centuries.
Life after life you have taught me;
since the cold, damp walls of caves
echoed my youngest voice, and
I was old in earlier years.
My teacher of all that was, is and ever will be,
you have shown eons of patience
with this irresolute child
dawdling on her way to school.
I am consumed by love. Your power
overwhelms me and lays bare my soul.
I feel your blessings seep into my depths;
your energy infiltrating me.
I feel a youthful nervousness.
I wait for that breathless moment
when you stretch out loving arms
and I melt into your warm embrace.
My Master of the higher realms,
I am humbled, this child of Earth.
I sit in the presence of divine wisdom
and feel a fountain of joy well up within me.

After Jeff died I was introduced to another spirit guide.

Sitting in my armchair, tears sliding down my cheeks, mind and body weary with grief's negative energy, I was suddenly transported into another space of mind and spirit. In front of me knelt a beautiful man. He had long hair pulled back from his face. His chest was bare and he was dressed in a pair of jeans. His hands rested on my knees. Light shimmered around him. From his eyes came great compassion and love.

"Who are you?" I asked. "What are you doing here? What do you want of me?"

With a clear, gentle voice he replied, "I am your brother, Little Eagle. We shared a lifetime together. I have come to help you through this period of grief. I will remain with you until you return home."

Little Eagle

Bare-chested, long black hair,
direct dark eyes, a wolf at your feet,
"Good morning, my brother."
Yes, I have known you before.
High up on a mountain
a rough-hewn timber cabin
snuggled among the trees.
From a cliff edge
you and I watched the bison
roam the valley far below.
The stream gurgled,
tumbled over rocks,
hurried on its journey
to the great river of the bear.
Gently you came to me
when the cold hands of grief
squeezed my aching heart,
when pain cramped my mind.
You held my hands.
You shared my pain
as you did in yesteryears.
Then I was your little sister.
It was I who died in your arms,
a child of seven
burning with deadly fever.
You buried my body;
piled stones around me.
The slow beat of your drum
set my spirit free.
Ah, those drums, my brother,
how they still speak to me, and
your presence the epitome of strength and love.

Spirit Guides cannot live our lives for us. My Master and Little Eagle could not rob me of my experiences, but they made my burdens much easier to bear. Through my despair, my grief, my loneliness, my struggle to start life again without my mate, they were there for me, surrounding me with love and helping me in practical ways to adjust, to stand strongly in my own power.

Guides are those unseen spirit beings who surround us, waiting for us to call upon them to guide us through the mire of our Earth experiences. They cannot walk our path for us. We chose our path before we returned to Earth's domain. For those who chose a tough road to walk, as I did, remember we chose it for good reasons. Our greatest lessons often come through suffering and pain. We were born with free will and we are the *only* creators of our life's journey.

Spirit Guides are as individual as you and I, as the birds of the air, the dolphins of the sea, beings from other planets and those of the cosmic realm. They come in many forms, and will appear to us in a manner that accords with our beliefs. They come in a way that is easy for us to accept. It is a joyous feeling to know that we are never alone. Help is just a word away, a prayer away. Unconditional Divine Love surrounds us every moment of our lives.

Chapter Eight - The Void

The Knife

My fist to the clouds,
the scream of grief
flung through the valley
and then,
curled in foetal form,
the forsaken child
upon the ground
sobs, rocks, moans.
Slowly
the woman returns,
sits up, blows her nose,
the flood of tears abating,
the old handkerchief saturated.
And in my heart dull pain
where the knife of death
has plunged its searing blade.

During the darkest period of my grief I had an experience that was quite frightening in its intensity. All I could see was a black abyss, emptiness, a void. The thought of returning home and joining my lovely Jeff was, in that instant, very appealing.

I remember being outside, screaming my pain to the clouds, sitting on the ground hugging myself and rocking back and forth. I curled up in the foetal position and sobbed until I felt totally exhausted and empty. In that moment I sat on the edge of the abyss looking into the blackness. There was no feeling, no thought, no reasoning. I was totally blank with no movement or sound, no colour, just a blank lifeless shell. Later I realised I had sat on the line between sanity and drowning my mind in the flood waters of grief.

Someone had looked after me and prevented me from sliding down into that abyss. When I eventually came out of it I was frightened by the intensity of my feelings to take the option of leaving and joining Jeff. I felt ill and extremely shaken by the experience. I realised I had come close to insanity or perhaps more accurately, to no mind at all. I came close to allowing my soul to break its connection with my body and this life. Trembling uncontrollably with shock, I staggered inside, climbed into bed fully clothed and slept.

When I woke night had fallen. The house was in darkness. Shivering, I rose, switched on most of the lights in the house, lit candles, had a hot shower and made a strong cup of coffee. I curled up in my favourite chair, wrapped in a blanket, and went back over what I had been through.

Gratitude welled inside me for my spirit guides having held me in that moment, for having stopped me from sliding into oblivion. It was a turning point in my grief. I thought about all the wonderful things I had in my life; my family and friends, my home, the beauty of the land and all the delightful creatures that were my constant companions, my health, the gifts with which I was born and the love of the Universe. I knew I still had a lot to do before it was time for me to leave.

Most of us, at some stage in our life, face the void. For people such as me it is a brief encounter. For others it is a place revisited, and for a few the void beckons so strongly they cannot resist slipping into it.

What is 'the void'? Simply, as the word suggests, it is that place of nothing. It is total emptiness. The void is within us. It is, in fact, the beginning of creation… our creation. In that place there is no thought, no feeling or movement. It is colourless. It is a place waiting to be filled with light and life.

In a home in India for the physically and mentally ill where I have worked, there was a woman called Elizabeth. Elizabeth had mentally entered the void. She had been traumatized during the Second World War to such an extent she no longer wanted to be part of this world. She had been a woman of high intelligence with an astounding scientific mind that had been used in underground service to her country. It was painful for me to watch this beautiful lady staring blankly into space, her movements slow and automatic. Elizabeth's soul hung on to her body by a very fine thread. She sat between two worlds, Earth and her soul home. She existed in the void. Painful as it was for me to watch her, for Elizabeth it was a place of safety where she could feel no pain.

I do not believe we are meant to enter the void. We have free will and it is our choice, but we came to Earth for a reason. We chose to come here. We have lessons to learn and work to do. We are here for the evolution of our soul. The void becomes what we make it. Because it is a place of 'nothing' it, therefore, has huge potential to be filled with the wonders of our own creations.

Lying on the ground, curled up in foetal position, I faced that void. I had to make a decision to mentally or physically enter that void, or to see it for what it was – an empty space between two worlds within my mind, a space waiting to be filled with love; my love, my colours and my light. At a subconscious or higher-self level, I knew I would not enter the void, but I had to experience seeing it to understand its place in my mind, my life, and the life of others.

The void is neither negative nor positive – it simply IS! It is a blank canvas upon which we paint our life, or the blank page on which we write our life's experiences. This blank canvas or page has huge potential to manifest whatever we wish to place there. The possibilities are endless. It is only our own thoughts that prevent us from creating that which we most desire.

Facing the void, for me, was the beginning of my new life.

Finding Joy

From out of my humanness I rise,
upward to the realms of my higher being.
Oh sweet, precious seclusion!
I share this intimacy with no-one.
This divine self is sensual bliss,
love welling within.
The flame of my inner candle
expands, explodes outward
till its light and the light of the cosmos
mingle, merge into oneness.
And the music, how it fills my body.
The energies of music and light
entwine with divine love.
Tears, unbidden, roll down my cheeks.
Complete is this joy that erupts
into the stillness of the night.

Chapter Nine - Three Stages

Wedding Anniversary

It rained last night.
Your ashes have gone.
The moss on the rocks is a vibrant green.
It is twenty-four years since you placed
this ring upon my finger.
My first bottle of sparkling wine
without you.
No shared spa-bath this year.
No dinner for two in front of an open fire.
Can you see the Erica?
My wedding flowers are in full bloom
as they always are this time of year.
Can you hear me?
Today I renew my promise
to respect, honour, love and trust you.
I wish I could kiss you!
It rained last night.
Your ashes have gone.

Some of the most difficult times following the death of a loved one are the anniversaries, birthdays and other celebrations. Our wedding anniversary was, for me, the first of such celebrations. It came just three months after Jeff died.

My friends, knowing this would be a difficult day for me, lovingly suggested activities to keep my mind occupied. They did not realise, in their concern for me, nor could they comprehend that the exact opposite was what my heart desired. It was not appropriate to block the pain associated with this celebration. There were times when I needed to be left alone to feel the full extent of raw emotions. I knew it was a vital part of my healing. I began to recognise the three stages in the healing process.

The first stage was the pain and the tears. When I counsel people now in grief healing work, one of the first things I say to them is, "Cry! Allow the pain to flow. Don't block it because you are afraid of what others may think or how they may react. If they are embarrassed that is their problem, not yours!"

When we lock pain away inside of us, when we block the rightful passage of tears, we store up within us by-products of pain, anger, resentment, jealousy, fear, and loneliness. There is little more draining mentally or physically than these negative emotions of the heart. There is nothing more damaging to our spirit, our soul, than the constant barrage of these emotions when we cling to the pain and don't allow it to be released. Our tears are the natural release of pain.

In the second stage, once my tears had been spilt and the pain felt, then came the hollow, empty feeling deep within. My thoughts slowed to a walking pace. A peculiar calmness would accompany this emptiness, along with the feeling of being totally alone, no matter how many people were with me. And, in truth, I was, in that moment, totally alone. I was meant to be totally alone for, as I eventually realised, the only person who could heal me was me. Others can give us tools to work with; they can give us love and support but, ultimately, we are the only ones who can move through our grief to find happiness. I saw clearly the choice was mine… stay stuck in my pain or learn to move on and eventually find happiness again.

In the third stage, meditation became a great tool. In the early stages of my grief, after the tears had been shed and I felt empty and hollow inside, I used to curl up and sleep. Eventually I saw what this stage was meant to be, a time to rest and allow peace to fill that hollow space. When I began to see the three stages clearly, instead of curling up in foetal position and sleeping, I would meditate. Through meditation I allowed that empty, lonely space to be filled with divine love and warmth.

A Meditation

Take the phone off the hook and turn off your mobile phone. Put on some soft flowing music. Light a candle or two. Sit or lie down in a relaxed way. Begin by taking deep, even breaths, slowly in and slowly out. With each outward breath let go of the tension and feel your body relax more and more. After you have taken six such breaths, concentrate on removing all the tension in your body. Begin with your feet and, step by step, work your way up to the top of your head. Note how much tension you carry in places like your back, your shoulders, the area of the jaw, your hands and the muscles of your abdomen. Note the thoughts that flow through your head. Allow them to enter and then drift away. When you feel your body totally relaxed, begin to visualize a bright white light surrounding your body. See this white light cocoon you. Imagine this white light cleansing you as water does when you bathe. Begin to feel the peaceful effect this relaxation and white light are bringing to you. Next, envisage a single shaft of white light moving down through the top of your head. Allow this white light to move slowly into your brain, down into your throat, then into the shoulders, down the arms, down into the chest and all the way to the tips of your toes. As this white light moves slowly and gently through you, it brings love, warmth and healing. Allow that feeling of divine love and warmth to expand and move into every muscle and organ, into your bones and even into your skin. When you have completely filled yourself with this white light, feel yourself surrounded by loving beings protecting you, watching over you and caring for you. Thank them for being with you and bask in their love and compassion. When you are ready, come out of meditation by taking some deep breaths, wiggle your toes and fingers, feel the firmness of your body and open your eyes slowly.

This is a simple meditation and you can expand on it as you gather confidence in yourself and your connection with the divine love of the universe.

The more I practised this meditation the stronger I became. Celebrations still brought tears to my eyes, still made me long for my mate, but I was more grounded and the length of time the pain lasted decreased. I was able to handle such celebrations as grandchildren's weddings, Christmas and birthdays with strength, grace and gratitude for the love of family and friends in my life.

Come Morning

Come Morning!
The night's rainstorm has passed.
The earth, fresh from the deluge,
will glow gold
with Sun's first kiss.
A hint of light
seeps into the darkness.
Come, Morning!
Let the birds sing
homage to the new day.
Come, Morning, come,
the deeds of darkness are done.
Shed the sable cloud
that enmeshes me.
Come, Morning, come!

Chapter Ten - The Healing Power of Nature

Jeff used to say, "Nature is the greatest doctor, the best psychologist." I have found him to be right many times since he left for higher realms. When it comes to healing the heart and the soul, nature is indeed a powerful healing force.

Tree Hug

Tree energy calms my aching heart,
accepts my tears on grey-brown bark.
A strong bent trunk
holds fast my weakness
against its twisted form.
This tree, scarred
by droughts and wild winds,
holds me to its breasts,
absorbs my pain.
From behind closed eyes
I see your face.
I feel your arms enfold me,
feel waves of warmth
flow through my body.
Yesterday I hugged a tree!

Trees, the earth and the sea possess great healing energy. They heal us when we are depressed, lonely, sad, angry, or have any other kind of negative emotion. Try hugging a tree, or lie back on the grass, or sit beside water, the sea, a lake, a river or a waterfall and feel the healing power of Mother Earth.

Trees take in gases that are poisonous to us and convert them into the life-giving oxygen we need to survive. Trees have a powerful field of energy giving out healing properties every moment of every day. For me they are a part of my life force. I cannot live without trees near me. When I enter the polluted air of cities I feel I am suffocating at a physical and spiritual level.

Hugging a tree can be a profound experience. Why not try it? Walk into a forest or a park. Stand still for a while and sense which tree to hug. The tree will call you to it. When you have found your tree, walk quietly up to it and wrap your arms around it. Still your thoughts! Forget what others will think. Relax and let your body rest against the tree. In your mind thank the tree for its healing energy. Close your eyes and imagine the tree and you becoming one. Feel your two bodies meld into each other. Visualize the life-force inside the tree rising up from its roots to the crown and moving into each leaf. Feel this energy being transported into your body, your mind, your heart through the bark. Allow yourself time to quietly absorb this beautiful healing energy flowing through you. Before you release yourself, thank the tree again!

Everything on this planet has a field of energy. The chair on which you sit, the bed in which you lie, the pencil that first wrote these words, my computer, stones, water and people... we all have fields of energy. We *are* energy. This energy is inter-connected. Every day of our life our energy fields are connecting with the energy fields of the things around us and with those of other people.

If it is difficult for you to find a tree, or if you prefer, lie down on Mother Earth. Lie on grass, sand or dirt. Go through the same procedure as you would with the tree.

Thank Mother Earth for her healing energy. Relax your body and feel it meld into the ground beneath you. Visualize healing energy move up from the core of the planet on which you lie. Allow that energy to enter your body. Again, give yourself time to absorb and enjoy this passage of energy into your whole being. As with the tree, you may feel tingling sensations as the energy interacts with your energy. Before you sit up, give thanks to Mother Earth.

I have always found the sea to be a wonderful place of healing. During the break-up of my first marriage, I often went to the sea to gather strength and feel its peaceful energy fill me. Interestingly, the last two days prior to Jeff's death were spent by the sea. We had taken our English visitors for a drive along Victoria's Great Ocean Road. Jeff was a sailor in his earlier years. He loved the sea almost as much as he loved his forests. Somewhere inside him he knew he had to see his beloved sea before he died. We returned home from the coast after dark on Wednesday and on Thursday morning he died. Looking back on those two days it seems to me now to have been more than just a re-connection with his sea. At the time, I was struck by Jeff's reaction as he bounded out of the car and, without a second glance at our visitors or me, headed straight for the sand and waves. Now I can see it was a time of cleansing and healing for his soul before it left his body.

There are several ways to connect with the sea. Sit on a rock and dangle your feet in the water; lie with your body in the shallow part of the water; sit or lie on the sand close to the water's edge. Again close your eyes and thank the sea for its cleansing, healing energy.

Allow the sound of the waves to wash over you. Let your thoughts drift away. If you are in the water feel it cleansing, healing you as it laps around and over you. If you are on rock or sand feel that energy move in and through you. Again, give thanks to the sea before you leave.

Another way I helped to heal myself was through physical work in my garden. I wrote to Jeff in my diary… my body aches! Hard physical labour has taken its toll on joints that are no longer young.

Yet my mind is satisfied and my spirit uplifted from its kneading of sorrow. All day I thought of you (as I bent, pushed, lifted) and felt your presence near. You often spoke of the healing power of nature. I feel now, as you once did, the peace, the calmness that comes when in contact with the soul of nature. When you used to return from bushwalking or digging in your garden, at those times when you hugged me, your love was mellow. Your gentle touch revealed your tender feelings, and your smile was like the first rays of early morning sunshine.

The Morning After

How quickly the night has passed.
The magpie's song, bell-like,
rings through the valley. Rising
from the deep sleep of exhaustion,
I feel the softness of Universal Love.
There is a calmness, a quiet,
strong resolve in my soul's depths.
There is a peace that resonates
with each life-giving heartbeat,
each intake of crisp morning air.
I listen to the forest's collective voice.
I feel the healing power
of Sun's winter rays
as it gently warms, thaws
the cold ache of despair.
And I know life is a joyous journey!

Chapter Eleven - The Source

Tears of grief have no respect for time or place. They often ran down my face at the most inappropriate times and usually without warning. I remember standing at a counter, waiting to have the registration of Jeff's car changed over into my name, silently crying. The man behind the counter was having great difficulty dealing with his embarrassing customer.

It was not the actual changing of names that brought on the tears. It was handing over Jeff's death certificate. At a time when I was struggling to cope with this sudden change in my life, the super efficiency of the business world with its coldly calculating, practical applications, I found distressing. Each time I had to hand over a copy of the death certificate, Jeff's name was removed from yet another piece of paper. It felt like these people were methodically taking another part of Jeff away from me. His name was being erased from computer screens and official documents, as though this lover of mine had never existed.

I knew the changing of documents needed to take place quickly, some, such as superannuation and bank accounts, within the first couple of days after he died, but it was a cold and heartless process. I struggled through it in a dazed state of mind feeling unbalanced and a fool.

A fool I was not, unbalanced I was. After that particular episode of crying, I got home and, cup of coffee in hand, thought about the embarrassment of the man behind the counter.

"Why can't I control these tears?" I asked. "Why do I feel so unbalanced?" A voice said, "Go to the source." Oh great! Go to the source? What source?

The Inner Voice

And the inner voice spoke.
"Yearn to know the power of your soul.
Feel its energy weaving thoughts
through the corridors of your mind.
Feel its breath give life
to the centre of your deeper knowing.
The voice of your spirit
is waiting patiently to be heard.
Make time to be still.
You crowd your days,
drowning hollowness with busyness,
afraid of the silence.
Be still and hear your soul
sing softly to your loneliness
a melody of love, far sweeter
than any you have known before.
Be still! Yearn to know
the wondrous power of your soul."

So the *source* was within me. It is within all of us. It is the very core of our being. It is our deeper, divine self; what I now call my 'god-self.' We all have this source of love, peace and strength. We may be ignorant of its existence and its power, or refuse to tap into it, but none the less it is 'there' within our being.

I was born with free will. It was my choice, my decision alone, to allow myself to go to that source and find the strength and courage to get through those wretched days, or allow myself to remain engulfed in my negativity of grief.

It is wholesome to allow the tears to flow, to allow the pain to be felt. It is a vital part of healing. The emotions need to be released. To push the pain down and put a lid on it, to keep it locked inside, or escape it in busyness, only prolongs our time of healing and can lead to physical or mental illness. However, pain and tears can also be addictive. Over the months that follow a loved one's departure, the time span between tears becomes greater and the pain becomes a little easier to bear.

We are not meant to live in a continuous state of despair. Our journey as humans is to find a road that leads to happiness and fulfilment. It is our responsibility… nobody else's… to seek out that road and, deliberately, a step at a time, move towards that goal. By tapping into the source of divine love within us, we can help ourselves speed up the healing within our hearts and minds.

How do we get to this source of divine love and strength? The first step is in accepting that we are more than flesh and bone; accepting that we are spiritual beings… one with and part of the universal energy, the eternal life force… we are eternal. The second step, once we have accepted that we are also soul beings, is to understand that we originate from the pure essence of love, joyfulness and peace. When we reincarnate into human form, our minds tend to forget our sacred origins. This Divinity remains within us and is the most vital part of our being. The third step, remembering who we truly are, requires us to become still and, through contemplation of our thoughts, feelings and creativity, we discover that pure essence, the beauty of our soul. When we discover the source, that beauty within our soul, we can then take the fourth step and tap in to its eternal and boundless supply of strength, love, compassion and courage.

The world around us, our guides, friends, family and counsellors can give us tools with which to work, but the real help is inside us. We are our own greatest healer.

University

The University of Earth
goes on teaching
philosophies and theories
for me, student of the soul,
to put into practice.
In time past, the voice of Divine Wisdom
whispered in sleepless dark hours.
And when the god of light
rode high, at noon, in his chariot of fire,
Wisdom watched to see what I had learned.
Through the bleakness of Death's loss
I have found perpetual life.
Through your absence
I have found your presence, and
the fullness of my own spirit.
The University's lessons are tough;
the subject of grief the hardest of all.
Yet through the relentless hours
when the candle burned, guttered and died,
I found me - a strong being of light!

Chapter Twelve

Letting Go

You often hear people say to the bereaved that their loved one would not want them to be unhappy. Sometimes this is said in order to relieve the discomfort of friends, but (be that the case or not) they speak a truth. Our loved ones on the other side do want us to be happy. They are in a place of peace and joy and they want the same for us.

The time had come for me to begin letting go of Jeff, to stop hanging on to what we had and to think about my future, what I was going to do with the rest of my life. I was fifty-four years of age and I knew I had many years of life left to complete what I came here to do.

Jeff's and my communication was such he came through loud and clear, as though he were talking on the telephone to me. I am now used to "hearing" people from the other side in my work as a medium, but none have come through with the clarity that Jeff did. There was no mistaking the sound of his voice for it was as it had always been.

Jeff's messages were not always soft and gentle. More than once did I get a deserved reprimand. Always it was delivered with the intention of helping me to get out of my misery and to move forward. The constant message was don't look back, live for the now and move forward.

It's not easy letting go of someone you have deeply loved for twenty-four years. In some peculiar way it brought about a feeling of guilt to let go and be happy. The idea of being able to do what ever I wanted, without being accountable to anyone except myself, was a foreign thought that needed time to grow and mature in my mind.

I felt caught between two worlds, the past and the future, the physical and the spiritual realm. Slowly I began to understand, this human form of mine had caught me in its seductive power. I began to see that the here and now, that life itself, is a time-warp, designed to allow the real me (my soul) to grow through the joy and pain of this human experience.

As I Wrote

As I wrote
you stood beside me
watching the words emerge,
watching my love slide from the pen,
watching my heart dance upon the page.
As I wrote
you stood behind me.
I felt the glow of you surround me,
the touch of your hands on my shoulders,
felt your immense love fill me and become a song!

As a soul there is no such thing as separation from those we love. We are connected to them for all of eternity. Jeff did not grieve for me. From the other side, his vision, his knowledge was far greater than mine. He could see the bigger picture I could not see. He knew we were not separated.

There was no denying I still missed him. At times the tears would well up without warning. But gradually, laughter came more readily, and the joyfulness of life was seeping back into my mind and heart.

I learned that in letting go of my need, my desire, to have Jeff with me in physical form, I had begun to draw him back in a profound way through our soul connection. I was learning that my heavy energy, heavy vibrations of grief and pain were blocking this connection. People in the spirit realm, without the baggage of a body or the force that keeps us grounded to Earth, have a much higher and lighter vibration than we do. It is not easy for them to lower their vibrations in order to contact us. Jeff came through to me with far more clarity and strength when my energy was lighter with peacefulness and happiness.

I may have lost his humanness, but at another level we were rediscovering each other. It was as though we were beginning a new love affair.

Opening

Opening
my thoughts, my heart to the Universal Soul,
to you.
Discovering
an infinite source of strength, of help
in you.
Seeing
beyond the here to the sacred energy
that is you.
Healing
my pain-torn heart with rays of light
from you.
Knowing
the unseen presence, the radiant happiness
of you.
Releasing
my fears, those obstacles to the soul, to be
with you.
Evolving
treading paths that lead
to you.

Chapter Thirteen - Selling Our Home

Letting go also meant removing from my life the physical connections we had. The process took four years and I learned many valuable lessons during that time.

One of the hardest decisions I had to make was to put our home up for sale. This was no ordinary home. In 1980 we had bought seven and a half acres of land in an isolated forest setting. Three acres of it was a cleared flat through which flowed a beautiful stream. The other four and a half acres were comprised of tree-covered sides of hills. The river flat snuggled into a small valley. In every direction from our house you looked to forested hills. Three sides of our land bordered government-owned forests. On the fourth side our only neighbour's house was on the other side of the hill. The stream ran just eighty metres in front of our house. Kangaroos were daily visitors and grew to trust us. The bird life was abundant and interactive with us. From time to time koalas would pass through our land. At night the possums would appear looking for their dessert of apple.

For eighteen years we had been in a world of our own, living in a lovely home we had built with our own hands. Selling this bit of paradise, in which so much of our love, work and commitment to the land and each other had taken place, was an extremely difficult and heart-wrenching decision.

However, apart from the risk of living alone in such an isolated and fire prone-area, the heavy physical work required to keep the home running efficiently was immense. There was also the knowledge that, if I did not leave, I could not move forward in my life. It would have been easy to close myself off and live with the memories, and allow my grief and the past to totally absorb me.

Whilst my heart was rebelling and saying no to the idea of selling, my soul was whispering, "You have a new life to live. You have work to do. You are an evolving being and must leave this place to complete the work you are here to do!"

The battle raged within me, heart against mind, common sense against emotional attachment, spirit against my humanness.

One day, in early morning meditation, I asked for a sign as to whether or not I should leave. I had shared my confusion with a dear friend. Around lunch time this friend rang and said, "Joy, I know you are having a battle in your mind about selling your home. This call is not to say you should sell. However, if you ever do decide to sell, I can introduce you to a very good woman who has built her real-estate business around environmentally caring people wanting to buy or sell homes and land."

I had my answer. I immediately rang the woman and she came out to visit me. As she drove away, I knew I had just made a life-changing decision. Yet again the tears streamed down my face as I faced the reality that this life was ending, that the major part of my physical connection to Jeff was about to be severed. Now there was not only grieving for my departed lover, but also the grief of leaving behind our beautiful home and all the joy that went into its creation. Thankfully, my son arrived to spend the night with me. How glad I was to be able to share the emotions raging in me with someone I trusted to hold my heart tenderly in his arms.

There was no sleep for me that night. I fought a war against doubts, fears, anger at Jeff for leaving me and the enormous responsibility of my decision. Where was I to go? What was I going to do with my life? What did the future hold for me? Little did I know then I was about to walk an amazing journey.

When dawn broke, I rose and made a cup of coffee. I took it back to bed. I sat looking through our French doors to the hill and forest beyond. Within me, I felt the calm after the night's struggles. Jeff's presence was incredibly strong in the room. It was as though he were sitting on the foot of the bed. His voice came through, "What you are going to will be just as beautiful as that which you leave behind."

Bitterly I laughed and said, "Who are you trying to fool?"

And then, as though he were showing me, I remembered the beauty and grandeur of the mountains of Nepal where we had trekked together. Looking out at the little hill just beyond our bedroom, I thought, "Yes! This hill is tiny by comparison and nowhere near as grand, but, in its own way, is just as beautiful as those snow-covered giants. So it will be with my new home!"

Sunset

I sit on the veranda,
a glass of wine in hand,
the day's work completed.
I watch the sun sink,
A slow-moving stone
into a pool of hills.
Red ripples spread
across the clouds.
I watch the birds frantically feasting,
before dark robs them of light, and
Night wraps its arms
around its old friend Earth.
Come close, my Love, come close.
Let me feel you near.
All day I have toiled
preparing our home for sale.
All day memories have slapped me
as I discard this and cling to that;
slapped my mind and heart
with the history of our love.
Come close and let me know
that history is a teacher, a guide
leading us into the future, our tomorrows
built on a solid foundation of yesteryears.
Like this sunset,
the work is drawing me
to the end of a day.
So much we gathered
around us, inside us.
So much of you permeates this place!
Leaving this home is a sunset
that ripples red tears through clouds of emotions.
Come close, my Love. Hug me!
Caress my skin with evening's breeze,
whisper to me your love
through the sighing trees.

All through the period of people tramping through our home and over the land, assessing, criticizing, discussing how they would change this or that, unaware of how they were stomping on all of my cherished memories, I felt Jeff's presence supporting me, holding me, loving me.

The day the people, who eventually bought our home, saw it for the first time was 31st of December 2002… New Year's Eve… the beginning of a new year. The day I signed the contract for its sale was 17th January 2003, exactly one year since Jeff died. The day I closed the door for the last time and drove away from our home, our life, was 29th April 2003, our 25th wedding anniversary. Were they coincidences?

For me, I came to believe, when letting go of any relationship, be it through death or with a living person, it is important to let go of all physical attachments to that person. Physical attachments seemed to me to be a mirror of emotional attachments. I did not need to do it all immediately, but gradually through a natural process, as I gathered strength, finding my direction in life, allowing my heart to heal, learning to stand strongly on my own, allowing my mind to open to new possibilities and my soul to awaken and evolve into its own spiritual and psychic power.

Over the span of four years I let go of books, Jeff's car, furniture, rings, paintings and many other items that had been specifically Jeff's. Each release was done with reverence, and with a prayer of gratitude for the life we had shared.

Leaving

Painfully – I am leaving our home.
Leaving this forest that has breathed its life essence
into my soul; this land that has taught me
when you reach out with love trust flows back to you.
Something of our shared love will always remain.
This home (like our marriage) built together,
each step thought through with patience and care.
This landscaping (your trees, my rocks) created
with joy and satisfaction – sharing
new growth, first blooms, nature's lessons.
I take with me only this:
memories of special moments,
my emotional awakening, my spiritual growth.
I take your deep love for this land, for me
sealed forever in my heart, my soul.
Yes, I am leaving, painfully, to begin my new life!

Chapter Fourteen - Is My Loved One Happy?

In my work as a grief healer and medium I am constantly asked, "Is my loved one happy?"

Jeff's mind and emotions had been traumatized by war. Before I met him, he had gone through insulin shock treatment and two lots of electric shock treatment, to try and erase the hellish images that rose up at the slightest provocation; images that haunted his dreams.

On many occasions I held him, as deep sobs of pain shuddered through his body. At times, this trauma caused him to do or say things he later regretted, adding guilt to guilt. Anger at the injustices perpetrated against the 'common' people, through political decisions, was a constant force that boiled just below the surface at gut level. When it erupted, it was a force to be reckoned with. This anger was difficult to subdue. It was almost an obsession. I knew it was a counter balance to the actions he was forced to take in war zones; actions he believed to be wrong.

During these episodes of war neurosis, Jeff would look into my face with glazed eyes and say, "I am a murderer."

No amount of rational talk about serving his country, and saving other lives, could dispel in him that single, potent and soul-damaging thought. In those hellish moments there was little I could do but hold him, love him and accept him for who he was.

So the same question arose for me after he died, was he happy?

The Photograph

That faraway look in your eyes, as though
you see something in the distance, beyond my vision.
Your face strong, yet soft, tender with love thoughts
rising from your heart. Behind it all
that haunted look etched with Trauma's pain.
Have they gone now, my Love, those memories
that haunted you? Images that raised beads of sweat
cold upon your skin, turned dreams into nightmares,
the scream of war caught in your tense throat,
your body shaking with renewed shock.
And the anger against injustice, the rebellion
against materialism, have they gone too?
What happens to the negative energy when death
slides the soul back to the source? Do we carry it
into another life, or is it dissolved in Universal Love?
You were a powerful being. Your emotions revealed
the deep passions within, which easily surfaced
when evoked. How your love welled up with
the smallest touch, my slightest hint of sensuality.
Where have those passions gone?
I feel your smile inside this heart of mine.
Often I see those blue-grey eyes
look deep within me. I cannot detect any more
that haunted look, nor feel the pain
behind the smile this photograph conveys.

A few months after Jeff died, I went with two friends to see four mediums (two from the United States of America, one from Canada and one from Britain) demonstrate their psychic powers to a crowd of fifteen hundred people in Melbourne, Victoria. It was a full day seminar.

In the first section after lunch, the lady from Canada pointed to me and said, "You have a question to ask me?" Shakily, I stood to my feet fighting back tears. I took deep breaths and asked, "Is Jeff all right? Is he happy?" She related back to me things that Jeff had watched me doing through the previous week... activities she had absolutely no way of knowing about. It was validation that Jeff was communicating through her. Then I was given the answer I sought.

"He says to tell you he is at peace."

Within me I knew it to be the truth. Peace flowed through me as though he had placed his hands on my abdomen and said, "See?" Loving warmth spread right through my being and gratitude overflowed in tears.

Since that seminar, my ability as a medium has developed and grown. Jeff has played a major part in that development. I had known about my ability to *tune in* to the spirit realm since I was thirteen, but I had never allowed its progress beyond that knowledge. Fear of what others would think held me back. Jeff knew I had this psychic ability, but it was foreign to him and hard for him to accept. He was afraid of it. Ironically, after that seminar, Jeff became my first teacher. He came through loud and clear, giving me messages and encouraging me to link in to the spirit realm.

It has been my privilege in the last few years to act as a link between the departed and the bereaved. During this time I have been given glimpses of the realm of Spirit.

It is my understanding that when the soul leaves the body, returning home to the realm of Spirit, the binding negative elements of our human experience disintegrate and we become beings of love and light. It is my understanding we go through a life review, acknowledging the things we have done well and looking at those things we could have handled better. It is not a time of judgement. It is a time of reflection, of learning from both our mistakes and our successes. It is a time of debriefing, during which we are surrounded by a great amount of love and compassion. It is a time for our soul to rest after its tiring journey on this planet... to connect to our lovely soul family... a time to be at peace and unconditionally loved.

I have *seen* Jeff walking, dancing or floating through energy fields of colour. Each colour seems to have a unique healing and rejuvenating quality to it. When this happens there is a wonderful feeling of joy, not only in and around Jeff, but also inside me. It is as though a memory has been awakened of the beauty of my soul's true home.

Home

Home is where you are.
I am here where dense energy
stifles full awareness of this ethereal soul of mine.
You are home
where beauty is abundant,
love flows in waves and joy sings in laughter.
This earth-life of unease and pain
has slipped away from you.
I know sweet peace now softens your powerful energy.
You are home in that glory of light and colour,
where lessons are of a different kind,
and relationships more splendid.
You will find it hard to return to Earth
and complete the work left undone, now that you
have sat once more at the Divine hearth of love.
Sometimes I long for home. When experiences
suck the life-force from the very heart of me,
my soul cries out to eternity.
Yet I know there is much to do.
I have a contract to fulfil
before my time is due to return home, return to you.

Now, for me, death holds no fear. For me it is but a curtain between life and life. That life which is beyond the curtain is indeed a beautiful one.

But then, so is this life. I returned to this life to learn valuable lessons for the advancement of my soul. I returned willingly to work, and to help bring peace and love to Earth. We live on a beautiful planet that needs our love and respect. I am here of my own free will, and only I have created the life I now live. All that I have experienced, negative and positive, I have drawn into my life and agreed to experience in order to learn and grow.

We cannot lay blame at the feet of other people or at the feet of God. We are the master creators of who we are and how we came to be that person. God, or Great Spirit (or whatever term feels right for you) the angelic realm, the Masters, our guides and our higher selves can all help us if we ask for help, but they cannot live our lives for us. Every single experience I have had, I have agreed to experience and every experience has been of my own creation.

Jeff and I had a contract to be together for over twenty-four years. During those years I learned valuable lessons by being with him, as he did by being with me. I knew he would die before me. I knew I had another life to live after he returned to his soul's home. At a soul level, I agreed to go through the experience of grief. In so doing, I awoke to a part of me that had been asleep, hiding behind its barrier of fear.

Incredibly, through Jeff's death I found new life and the joy of reconnecting with him in a way we had never been able to share as husband and wife.

Chapter Fifteen - After The Shift

When I put our home on the market to be sold, I looked around for land on which to build my new home. I knew I had to build and not buy an established home. It was part of my healing to leave behind the past and to create a home that was entirely of my own making… a home that contained only my energy in its creation. It was a massive step in learning to stand in my own power. I learned to listen to the well-meant advice of family and friends, smile and say thank you, and then do what I felt I needed to do without getting caught up in other people's ideas or fears.

Within two years of Jeff's departure, I had sold our home, bought land and commenced the building of my new home. A home designed by me. Organizing finances, dealing with real estate agents, builders and associated companies and dealing with tradesmen challenged my faith in myself and my faith in my spirit guides. Through it all, I discovered an inner strength and abilities I did not realise I had.

My connection to my guides grew stronger and moved into a more deeply personal relationship. My heart was continuously filled with gratitude and love for them. Daily, I saw their helping hands at work in my life.

I rented a house in a small town close to where my new home was being built. I remember waking the first morning and feeling the impact of other houses so close to me. The sound of cars, mothers yelling at their children and sirens blaring was a challenge. I thought, "What in the hell am I doing here?"

The only sounds I was used to hearing were those of native birds giving voice to their beautiful songs at dawn, and the sound of wind in the trees. I lay for some time listening to the sounds of a small country town waking up with first light. Dogs barked, sheep bleated, introduced birds squawked or chirped, and in the distance, the sound of cows as they made their way to milking sheds. Trying to gather a more positive attitude, I mumbled, "I guess they are a part of nature too."

My heart yearned for the beautiful land and home I had left behind.

"Well," I thought, "I had better get over this, get out of bed and drive to my new land and begin bonding with it." There was no going back. I had to move forward. Then Jeff's words came back to me, "What you are going to will be just as beautiful as that which you leave behind." I dressed, filled a thermos flask with coffee, grabbed fruit, cheese and bread, then drove to my new land.

I had bought ten and a half acres of forested land. As I walked on to it, three kangaroos quietly hopped past me. Kangaroos were Jeff's favourite animals. Because of the structure of their hind legs and large tail, kangaroos cannot move backwards; they can only move forwards and when they do it is with great strength and speed. I knew it was Jeff's way of encouraging me to place that which we had shared in the past where it belonged and, like the kangaroos, move forward with strength. I spent the day discovering the beauty of my new land. I spent time meditating to the sound of native birds and the wind in the trees. I left at the end of the day knowing I could handle, for a short time, the rented house and the challenges it presented to me.

I was soon to discover that my neighbour was a drug dealer and frequently visited by the police.

On the other side of that neighbour was a hotel. Friday and Saturday nights stretched the boundaries of my sanity. Drunks roared their cars as they drove down the street, threw empty bottles and cans into my back yard, vomited into my front garden, and the hotel blasted out loud music until the early hours of morning. It was a rude contrast to my past.

Yet, whilst I was in that house for fifteen months, again I learned valuable lessons, lessons that were very different from any previous ones. Such was the trust in my spirit guides that at no time did I fear for my safety. I learned patience, trust, endurance and courage and that, even in the midst of chaos, I could find peace. My music became of utmost importance to me. I drowned out the ugly sounds beyond my walls with its beauty. Through the music I was able to connect to the deeper aspects of my mind, heart and soul.

The Lark Ascending

Composer: Vaughan Williams
The music penetrates,
and with the lark
I ascend to that other realm.
The passage between
my human and higher self
bridged, filled with music.
Each rising note
draws me through space,
through timeless ether
till the clouds' carpet
fades far below and
the call of the bird is silenced.
I see the abundance of all
that is within and around me.
I *know* the pure essence
of the Eternal Mind.
I feel the flood of joy
beyond all understanding.
I am that *I,*
total simplicity,
pure throbbing energy.
Enfolded within a spinning
coloured ball of light, I see
the rainbow of my soul.
And then the downward pull.
The music ends. I am drawn back
to the sound of a car door's slam,
the insistent ring of a phone,
the crackle of a wood fire burning
within this base, my earthly home.

I have always loved music and I had been a singer in my younger days. I had come from a rich background of music. In this peculiar setting, in this small town, I realised how much I had taken music for granted. For the first time, I had truly begun to understand the healing qualities of music, and I began to see how it can put us, quickly and beautifully, in touch with our deeper spiritual being.

Chapter Sixteen - Jeff's Poems

Whilst I was writing the poems for this book, I had been very aware of Jeff's presence. He seemed to be watching over my shoulder. On a number of occasions I asked, "Do you approve Sir?" During our marriage, whenever I wrote, he would come up behind me, place his hands on my shoulders, kiss the top of my head and ask me if I wanted a cup of coffee. Making coffee was rather difficult for him now, but he still let me know that he was watching and supporting me. At times, I felt a pressure on both my shoulders as though he had placed his hands there, as he always used to do.

Jeff was a lover of poetry. Often, after the evening meal, he would sit in his favourite chair, a glass of red wine in his hand, and read aloud from a much loved author's book of poems. Many a night I have watched him entertain guests with his readings.

He was my greatest critic and supporter as I struggled to break through into the world of publishing. His comments on my work (not always what I wanted to hear) were invaluable. For quite some time after he left me I felt unanchored without his input into my work. Because of him, my poetry grew and matured. He encouraged me to explore different avenues of getting my work known by the public. He knew of my conviction that poetry can be a form of healing for both writer and reader. He knew that my drive to write poetry was a way of reaching out and touching the lives of people, loving them through written words.

I often teased Jeff, telling him that he was a poet too. One day, during meditation I asked him to connect with me. I had placed a pencil and blank pages of paper beside me. When I felt his presence, I asked him to write, through me, a poem for this book. He began to dictate. I had no knowledge of what was being given to me until afterwards, when I read through what had been written. I was too busy trying to keep up with him. Words came at a rapid rate. I had to concentrate on getting the words down without thinking about what he was saying. When he had finished and I looked at the scrawl in front of me, I realised there were, not one, but two poems.

It was the first time I had acted as a channel for the written word. I was excited and in awe of what had just happened. I knew what an effort it was for him to bring the poems through to me. I felt humbled by the experience and proud of him.

"See," I cried, "I always knew you were a poet!" I felt him smile.

The following poems are as Jeff gave them to me.

Poem One

Let music fill your life.
Through its strains
you connect with the joy of heaven.
Let the vibrations of your soul
be lifted to a higher plane
with each note, each beat.
Remove the blockages of grief.
Come out of darkness into light.
Only then can you and I work as one.
In the darkness of pain your vibrations dim.
Let your light shine
to help heal the grief of man.
Let your soul rejoice.
The colours of the heavenly dome
light your divine flame.
Feel it burn within.
Let the colours become one
until the light banishes all darkness.
Rise up from your seat of pain.
Stretch your arms to the Universe.
Breathe in the breath of love.
Fill your soul from the Divine fountain.
Let the waters cleanse away all fear,
for you are a wondrous child of God.

Poem Two

A little while I am gone from you!
A little while and I will return.
The mountains rise and valleys form.
The seas erode the shores.
All of life is in constant change.
So must you, so must I change.
We are evolving
children of the Universe.
There is no death.
We create a vehicle
and ride through time
enclosed in its form.
You saw me leave my vehicle.
You sensed my joy in release.
What you are in this human form
is but a part of you.
You feel my presence beside you.
Overwhelming love flows
over you, through you.
You almost see my spirit being.
You know the vibrational tingling
as I touch your energy with mine.
This, then, is the real me, the real you;
this field of energy, this light.
When I return
the child will be a small part of me.
The greater you, the greater me
remain forever connected.
I will not leave you, nor do I wish to.
Our love is boundless,
beyond all earthly knowledge.
We are united through Divinity!

Chapter Seventeen - Time Out

Some months before Jeff died we had, what was for me, a disturbing conversation. Jeff made a statement that I should remarry were he to die. I told him not to be foolish. How could I possibly entertain the thought of another man in my life when I was so much in love with him? He wanted to know what I would do.

"Why are we talking about this?" I snapped. "What's this all about? For God's sake, we have still got a lot of living to do together. If you must know, I will put all of my energy and love into writing. I don't want to hear this talk of another man again." He looked at me with sadness in his eyes; a type of sadness that made me very uncomfortable. He was acknowledging what I feared to face; our time together was drawing to a close. I returned his gaze with moist eyes and simply said, "How could I ever love another man after what you and I have shared?" "Well, I want you to," was his reply. It was never spoken of again, but it hung in the air between us.

About a year after he died, well-meaning friends began to make suggestions that perhaps one day I might meet another man. I felt affronted by their comments. Didn't they understand how much I loved, and still loved, my husband?

It was far too early in the grief process for me to even contemplate the idea. It was like they were treading all over our twenty-four years together with very muddy boots. It stirred up anger and I became defensive of my love for Jeff. The more it was spoken of, the more I rebelled and the angrier I became. Throughout the next year, from time to time I would be asked, "Will you marry again?" In the end I would shrug my shoulders and reply, "Who knows?" I just wanted them to shut up and leave me alone. I felt that our holy of holies had been violated. A couple of men had made a move towards me. My response to them was one of disgust. I thought, "How crass you are, how insensitive. Do you think I have suddenly become an available object to be repossessed?" Later, I recognized that what they were doing was preparing the ground for what was about to happen.

For me, the love I had shared, and still shared with my mate was incredibly strong. The connection we had through the spirit realm was powerful. I had been keenly aware of his help and influence in all that I had done since he had left for his spiritual home. Rather than a waning of love, the love had increased and strengthened. His presence was strongly with me at all times.

Dream Lover

Come to me, comfort me
while embers die to blackness.
Protect and hold me
to your ardent heart.
As the world recedes into ebony
and the moon climbs stairs
to her highest balcony,
wrap me in the silence of sleep.
Stars trek across the cosmic realms.
Come to me, my dream lover,
weave your magic into my heart.
Whisper only those things
the night can tell.
The goddess casts silver light
to where I lie, restlessly waiting
to feel your velvet kiss.
These hours are mine alone,
except for you, my invited guest.
You who slides into my mind and
beckons me to your gossamer arms.
My phantom man of the night,
who lingers seductively in memory
when dawn cowers night to the west,
and I am alone once more.

One morning, as I was busily doing housework, Jeff's voice came through strongly to me.

He said simply, "Another man is coming into your life."

"No!" I shouted.

Silence followed. Then about six months later it happened again during meditation.

Again I shouted, "No! Don't do this to me. How can you say such a thing?" Again I was met with silence.

Early in June two thousand and five, three and a half years after Jeff's departure, I became very ill with a dose of influenza. I was in bed for six days. I asked others not to visit me because I did not want to pass on this wretched virus. I was extremely weak, had dreadful headaches and my whole body ached. I flipped from being very hot to being very cold. It became one of the greatest blessings I had been given. It gave me time out to think and feel through a lot of stuff I had kept buried beneath business. There was nothing I could physically do. I had hours, between sleeps, to come to terms with a lot of deep-rooted grief I had been avoiding.

All too often we human beings bury our pain beneath busyness. It does not serve us well. Eventually pain has to be faced, one way or another. It festers inside us until it erupts into depression, a mental breakdown or a physical ailment of some kind. For me, my body took charge and said, "Enough of this hiding, it's time to face up. I won't do too much damage to you. A good dose of the flu should just about fix it."

I began to understand that letting go of someone has many layers. It is these inter-twining layers that cause the confusion that ebbs and flows in our feelings. How many times had I said, "But I thought I had let go of him!" In fact, what I had been doing was peeling back the layers of grief, not realising how many layers there were to deal with. The bigger test was still to come.

I was beginning to understand that I not only had to let go of the physical Jeff but, more importantly, I had to let go of the spirit of Jeff… not only for my sake, but for Jeff as well. And there-in lay the deepest confusion and the deepest grief that I had tucked away beneath my busy life.

I realised that in encouraging our spiritual, psychic contact I had not truly let go of him. In not letting go of him, I was binding him to me and stopping him from moving on and doing what he needed to do. Lovely as the contact had been for us, it was time for both of us to stand alone. Never have my tears been so copious. I ran out of tissues and started using toilet paper.

Eventually I faced the question; if a man came into your life, Joy, that you felt attracted to, what would you do? How would you feel? Every part of me screamed NO! I meditated to try to still my thoughts and gain an honest answer. I should have guessed what was about to happen. My man's voice came through loud and clear. This time there was no arguing. This time it was like a kick in my rear.

"There is another man coming into your life. Do not reject him. Do not turn away from him. He is coming to help you and you were destined to meet."

Within me, I screamed, "Why? I have you. I don't need anyone else. It is you I love, and only you. I do not want involvement with another man."

"You must let go of me. This man is important to you. You must accept him into your life. You need him and he needs you."

I spoke to a dear friend I trusted and told her what had happened. Mary intuitively pressed the right button.

"It seems to me," she said, "that you are feeling a sense of betrayal to Jeff if you find another man appealing."

The flood gates opened. From deep down, hidden beneath logical thoughts, coated over with independence and with a big spoonful of strength dobbed on top… there rose up yet another layer to the mud cake of grief. As the tears flowed, I nodded my yes. That sense of betrayal to my beautiful man, betrayal of his love for me and my love for him, was like a volcanic eruption welling up from somewhere oh-so-very deep down.

I muttered to myself, "Will these tears never end? When do the tears stop? And how can I let go of him? He has said we are together for all of eternity. So how can I let go and still be connected to him?"

Then the still, small voice, that voice that comes when the tears have all been shed, that tiny voice that is heard in the dark hours of night, that voice said, "Let go of your dependence upon him, as a child lets go of the hands of its parents and learns to walk alone. He will still be there for you, as the parents are there for their child… even after the child has left home, found a job and a partner. The love of the parent does not lessen for their child, nor does the child's love lessen for its parents. But the child must let go of that hand and walk its own path.

In meditation, I went to my man. I took his hands in mine. I vowed to love him for all of time. I asked him to be there for me when I returned home. I told him I wanted to share another life with him in our next reincarnation, to complete what was not done in this lifetime. And then… I let go.

Again I experienced that incredible pain of grief for which there is no physical analogy. I wept. The tears abated. I felt hollow inside.

And then his voice, soft and loving, flowed through the ether to me. "You know I will always love you. Yes we will be together again. We are bonded spirit to spirit. But you have an earth life to live. And this is not just about you. The man who is coming to you needs your understanding, your compassion and your love. He will be there to help you, and you will be there to help him. It is your destiny. Go with my blessings, and know my love for you will never diminish, nor will I ever leave you."

Who knew what lay ahead for me? All I knew was that I had let go of his hand. With a humbled heart I said, "Not my will, Great Spirit, but thine!"

I thanked the virus for the blessings it had given me by sending me to bed. It gave me days where I could no longer hide another layer of grief beneath busyness, logic, independence, strength and devotion to Jeff.

To this time of writing, that man has not appeared. It matters not. When the time is right, he will walk into my life and I will love him as much as I loved Jeff. I will not turn away from him. Joyfully, I will accept him into my life. Until then, I have a lot of work to do helping others to move forward with strength and courage; helping them to let go too, and discover that life is a joyous journey!

Chapter Eighteen – Stepping Into My Power

Steep Climb

You loved to climb mountains.
You would stand at the top, hands on hips,
panting, your lungs sucking in sweet air.
Your heart pounded with exhilaration,
while your eyes scanned the horizon.
It was your way to rid yourself of pain,
to drink nature's beauty deep into your soul and
erase the babble of thought that tumbled in the mind.
This isolation from mankind, this stillness and peace,
was a balm that glowed through your eyes.
There, on the mountain top,
you were one with the Universal Spirit.
For me, this climb never seems to end.
When I believe I am almost there,
another ridge appears, another damn challenge.
Sometimes I feel lost, weary, and must rest,
filling my delicate cup from the healing stream of tears.
Sometimes I close my aching eyes and let
the shadows, the breeze, cool my tired spirit.
Often the climb is painful, but when I reach the summit
I will see you… waiting… strong arms outstretched,
waiting for me to share that wondrous eternal view.
There, on the mountain top,
I will be one with the Universal Spirit.

After experiencing the influenza virus, I felt a shift begin to happen in my contact with Jeff. There was not the same intensity there had been. Initially it brought up feelings of insecurity.

Jeff no longer came through as frequently. I felt the connection was beginning to fade and I was fearful of losing altogether the contact that had been my life-line and my support.

As the weeks progressed, I received a constant and simple message from my friends. Eventually, I realised it was my Master's way of getting the message through to me. Comments such as, "I admire you. You have so much strength to have done what you have," and, "You've got a lot of guts to do all this alone," or, "You're a powerful woman Joy," and, "Joy, where did you find the strength to do all this so quickly?" I always replied that I had been given a lot of help. At first I accepted their comments as nice compliments but, after a time, I began to wonder at the repetitiveness of the comments. Sometimes it takes a while for our minds to really grab what is being said.

Our spirit guides, the masters and the angels are wonderfully patient beings. They will bring a message to us over and over again until we eventually **get it**. I have this wonderful image at times of my guides sighing, looking at each other, shrugging their shoulders and saying, "Oh well! Eventually she will get the message."

These messages come to us in many different ways. The spoken word (as it was this time with me) the written word, through songs, cards, a feather placed on our path. A particular bird or animal constantly placed in front of us, directly through our thoughts, or through repetitive events. The list is endless. It is our job to be alert and to recognize the messages that come from our spirit guides.

One day, sitting on my veranda having a cup of coffee with a friend, she made the observation that I had done a lot in such a short time. I looked around at what I had achieved. Then finally the message sunk in! The message was… what *I* had achieved. And how had I achieved all this? With a lot of help from Jeff and my spirit mates… yes, but they could not have done a damn thing unless I had been willing to take the steps to make it happen. The message my spirit guides had been trying to give me was that my real support, my real strength lay within me, not out there in the ether.

Within us all is our god-self, higher self, our soul, our divine spirit, call it what you will. We are beautiful, powerful beings who have a well of strength and courage waiting for us to tap in to. It is our choice whether we remain in a place of weakness, or own and accept our power, and are willing to stand in that power. We can allow our thoughts to overrule our power, telling ourselves how we are weak, or we can step into our own beautiful light and see ourselves for who we truly are. We were created with this inner power base. It is a natural part of us.

Scientists tell us we only use five to ten percent of our brain's potential. Now there's a thought. If I felt I had achieved a lot since Jeff had died, how much more would I have achieved if I had kicked the other ninety-five percent into action? It was time for me to acknowledge my power, the strength that everyone else had been trying to tell me I had. It was wonderful having Jeff's help, but I really did not need it. I was quite capable of standing alone. That is what he was trying to say to me when he told me I had to let go of him. He would always be here for me, as will my spirit guides, my Master and all those other wonderful beings. They are willing to help when I ask. But within me I was already God incarnate, as we all are. When we begin to grab hold of that concept our insecurities begin to lessen.

We human beings can be so honest about the negative side of our nature, why, then, do we find it so difficult to be honest about our positive side? I am not talking about puffed-out chests, the "I'm better than anyone else," ego-based feelings that actually come from a place of insecurity, a need to convince ourselves that we are worthwhile. This is simply about honestly accepting that we are created beautiful beings… each unique with our own wonderful gifts and talents. When we begin to see, accept and own our strength and power, it is then our responsibility to use those attributes to work from a place of love, joy and peace, to use that power for the betterment of self and our **fellow** human beings. And the greatest power we have is the power of love.

Be Not Afraid

Be not afraid to love,
for love is the sun's rays
that open the bud of your heart,
gently exposing the beauty
of your most precious bloom.
Be not afraid to give,
for in the giving
love returns to you
in greater measure,
on the sound waves of a song.
Be not afraid of death
for it is but a curtain
between life and life.
In your deepest sorrow
may come your greatest knowing.
Be not afraid of life,
for in the vastness of the Universe
lies the greatest love,
the greatest compassion,
and boundless power waiting for you to....
Open the portals
of your mind, your heart,
that you may see beyond this earth-life.
Feel the pure radiant essence of that love
warm the depths of your soul.

Chapter Nineteen - Soul Mate

One month after releasing Jeff through meditation, I met a very lovely man. Nothing came of our meeting, but I gained from the experience knowledge that I was capable of loving again.

It was the first time such feelings for someone had surfaced. To begin with, I was shocked by the intensity of sensuality his presence evoked. It had been a long time since these emotions had been stirred within me. I had believed, after Jeff's death, that I would never feel those kinds of feelings again. Our sensuality, our sexuality and love had been such that I did not believe it was possible for me to love another man, and here I was feeling the rapture of being in this man's presence. I felt I had stepped backwards into my teenage years as I opened up to, and explored the possibility of entering into another loving relationship. Jeff's words came back to me, "Go with my blessings, and know my love for you will never diminish, nor will I ever leave you."

Cinderella

I sit at this table sipping red wine,
my meal washed down
with the pepper of shiraz.
It's noisy! The restaurant is full
of chattering shoppers, except for a few
like me who, with envy, dine alone.
How special it would be to see you
walk through the door, the smile
in your seductive eyes, on your sensual lips.
I cannot believe I feel this way!
Cinderella waiting to become a princess,
but the pumpkin carriage is drawn by rats.
It's time for me to return to my hearth.

It is now my belief that we have more than one soul mate. For me to understand this thought there was a question I needed to answer. What is a *soul mate*?

I knew that my relationship with Jeff had gone beyond the mind, heart and body. He was my soul mate. But this definition of one's partner being a soul mate, what did it truly mean? To talk of the soul, for me, meant moving beyond thoughts and emotions to the spiritual being, the soul being, that part of us that never dies and returns to its soul home when it leaves its vehicle, the body. Therefore, to call someone my soul mate, I needed to know them at a soul level, spirit to spirit.

The best way I can describe this kind of connection is, when I have met someone for the first time and feel as if I have known them for years. I probably have, for centuries in fact, in other lifetimes on Earth or in other realms. There comes with the connection an instant feeling of warmth, excitement and a sense of *knowing* that person. But, for the person to be our special lover, our *mate* at a soul level, I believe that our past connection must have been of a very close and intimate nature.

I believe there is a difference between a soul friend and a soul mate. I have many soul friends in members of my family and my dear friends, with whom I know I have shared past lives, but I don't want to be their lover. So what is the difference?

A soul mate brings with them the added attraction of in-depth intimacy. Something you would share with your mate but would not share with anyone else, physically, mentally, emotionally and spiritually. There is a level of trust, a *knowingness* that goes beyond the simple sharing of thoughts and emotions. There is a feeling of security, of safety in that lover's presence and the deep desire to give, receive, share and care. There is to the relationship a feeling of 'we've been here and done this before and it's nice to be doing it again.'

I shared some lovely moments with the new man who had stepped into my life but, in the end, I knew he was not a soul mate as Jeff had been with me. He knew it too and so we have remained good friends, soul friends. He gave me a wonderful gift, the knowledge that I was capable of loving again. Through him I have been able to prepare my thoughts and my emotions for the possibility of meeting another soul mate. And thus began another level of learning to let go.

With the awakening of my passion came the hunger to be loved. To feel a man's arms around me, to share all life has to offer, and the desire to laugh together. But also, with the realisation I was capable of loving again, came the loneliness.

Chapter Twenty - Dropping into Silence

Our spirit guides speak to us in different ways. I have learned to differentiate between my thought patterns and those of my guides. When my spirit guides speak to me through my thought waves it is a telepathic communication. The closest simile I can find is listening to music through headphones with the volume turned down low. When you listen to music in such a way, the sound is not external, but rather seems to come from inside the head.

Once you look for such telepathic communication and recognize it, you begin to understand the subtle differences between your own thoughts and the voice of your spirit guides.

We are all capable of such communication, not only with our guides but also with each other. How often have you said to someone, when they have voiced a certain thought, that you were thinking exactly the same thing? For example... if I were to say to myself that I would like to go to the sea for a swim, and then a friend of mine says, "Let's go to the sea for a swim." I would look at my friend and say, "How did you know that's what I was thinking?" Without realising what we were doing, we would have been telepathically communicating. It was a form of communication that Jeff and I frequently experienced.

When couples are closely attuned to each other, it is a common experience to pick up on each others thoughts. I believe cats and dogs are experts at such communication.

Each thought you have goes out into the cosmos and is 'heard' by your guides. When we begin to understand this process, we also begin to understand what wonderfully compassionate, loving and forgiving beings they are. Think about all the negative rubbish we are capable of putting out into the ether through our thoughts. All the times we have blamed them for the experiences that have been of our own creation; all the pain and indulgence in self-pity for which we have blamed God and our spirit guides. My guides are amazing beings with a huge amount of patience.

When we learn to drop into silence, allowing the clamouring of the mind to slow down and take a more positive journey, we find our deeper self and develop a greater communication with our spirit guides. When I began to find my deeper self, by dropping into silence, I also began to learn what self-love truly meant.

Self-Love

Love begins with self!
You were love
before you were born.
You are love when you return home.
Between birth and death
you *are* love
within the very core of you.
Why, then, do you search for love
when it already dwells
within the depths of your being?
As sure as the sea tide turns,
when you learn to love self
love will flow back to your shore.

So what do I mean by dropping into silence? I hear you ask, "How can I be in silence when my head is full of the constant chatter of thoughts?"

The silence of which I write is not that silence of soundlessness. It is an inner experience. The secret in stilling your thoughts, to allow the inner peace of silence to feed your soul, is not to fight against your thoughts. Instead, become an observer of your thoughts. Allow them to flow in and then gently let them go. The more you consciously practice noticing and then letting go of your thoughts, the quicker your mind will still itself. The quieter you become inside, the quicker and easier you learn to drop into silence where 'the peace that passes all understanding' exists.

Try seeing your thoughts as a play, a story being acted out inside your head. Most of our thoughts have no real substance to them. A lot of our thoughts come from a base of fear…what if she says so and so; what if they don't like me; what if, what if. When you begin to see that the majority of your thoughts have no substance to them, when you begin to let go of your thoughts, you can step out of the fear into the stillness, the peace and drop into the silence.

A Meditation

Light your candles. You may wish to do without music for this meditation. If you do decide to have music, make sure your music is turned down low and preferably of the repetitive kind, such as chanting. Some modern classical pieces, like Phillip Glass' work, are ideal for this meditation, or some of the new age music. The music must not dominate in this meditation. Sit in a comfortable position. Take in several slow, deep breaths. With each inward breath, breathe in positive energy. With each outward breath release all tension from your body. As in the previous meditation, scan your body for areas of tension. Begin relaxing your body, starting with your feet and work your way up to the top of your head. When your body is fully relaxed, concentrate on your thoughts. Become an observer of these thoughts, as though you are almost separate from them. As each thought appears, allow it to drift through and let it go. Make no judgement about it. Simply let it drift in and out like waves lapping against a shore. After a few minutes, move from observing your thoughts to the sounds you can hear – cars, birds singing, the tick of a clock, the wind in the trees. Again be an observer of these sounds without naming them. If you hear a car, don't think, "Oh, that's a car." Be detached. Hear the sound without acknowledging what it is. By being an observer of sounds in this way, you begin to still the chatter in your head. Once you have observed the sounds around you, begin to hear the sounds within you – tummy rumbles, the sound of swallowing, heart beat, ringing in the ears, your breath. Again remain detached. Hear them without giving them a name. Observe that your thoughts have slowed down even further and have almost disappeared. Visualize a gentle flame, like that of a candle, burning softly in the centre of your abdomen. Concentrate on this flame. As you do, you become aware that even the sounds are beginning to disappear. This flame is at the core of your being. This flame is the essence of you, your divine self, and the source of all your strength, peace and love. Once you see the flame and can hold it with your inner vision, allow the flame to slowly expand. Let its light and warmth fill your whole body. See it moving outwards until it surrounds you in a cocoon of light. By now your chattering of thoughts has stilled and you have dropped into that inner silence. Here, peace is like a deep, still lake mirroring the beauty of your soul. Here, in this place of silence, you are the '*I AM*' – I am everything and I am nothing, I AM that which I AM. In this place of silence is your well of strength, courage and love. Allow yourself to enjoy being in this silence. When you are ready reverse the process. Become aware of the sounds within you and around you. Come back into the awareness of the room. Feel the chair in which you sit. Wriggle your toes and fingers. Take a deep breath and let it out slowly. Open your eyes.

If you have difficulty in moving through these steps, it may help to record this meditation technique onto tape, playing it back to yourself as you meditate. For some people visualization is difficult. If you cannot actually *see* the flame or light then simply sense its presence. The more you practice this meditation, the more you will become in touch with your true and beautiful self, and the quicker you will drop into silence. Eventually, you will be able to do this for just a few moments, throughout the course of your normal working day, by simply closing your eyes and allowing yourself to drop into silence

The more you drop into silence, the stronger will grow your connection to your spirit guides. The stronger grows your connection to your guides, the more aware you become of the love and help that surrounds you every minute of your life.

Chapter Twenty One - Karmic Law

Shrouded in Moonlight

Softly moonlight
falls on my nakedness.
I feel the pang of love's separation.
The cool night air
slips through the open window,
caressing my breasts, my thighs.
I sigh, longing to feel your body
filling in the curves of mine.
I long to feel your breath
tracing the contours of my face.
This yearning,
this hunger to know you
consumes
the minutes of my days.
I lie in the moonlight
crying quietly,
unable to sleep.
I call out to you,
"Does this pain
dwell in your heart too?"

As is often the case for people who find themselves alone after being in a relationship there comes a feeling of isolation when in the presence of couples. I felt this isolation strongly when I separated from my first husband before I met Jeff. It did not concern me for the first three years after Jeff left. I was too deeply in a state of grief, and anyway I knew he was still with me. It was rather like me and my invisible husband dining out with other people.

It was not until after I had released Jeff, and my encounter with the other man came to an end, did this feeling of isolation begin to have its effect. Why then? The desire to share with that special someone had been pushed to the surface. Being with couples brought the constant reminder that I was alone. Quite often widowed people, or those newly separated, go into a reclusive state of mind. They sometimes feel less isolated being at home alone than being out with others and, therefore, having to cope with the feelings of hurt, jealousy and resentment that can arise when seeing couples relating in a close way. For me, each touch, each smile they shared triggered a deep ache for what I did not have.

We are part of the natural laws of this planet. Mateship is one aspect of those laws; not only for the procreation of the species for survival, but also survival through communication and the sharing of responsibilities. The majority of our human race needs love and communication with a mate.

We are never too old to find another mate. During my years as a nurse, an incident happened within the hospital where I was working that had a profound effect on my young mind. A gentleman of eighty-four was recuperating after an operation. One of his orders from his doctor was to gently walk. He was told he could wander around the hospital providing he did not get in the way of the hospital staff and their duties. He would wander into the ward, where I worked, for women patients with non- operative complaints. He met a lady of eighty-five years who was recovering from a nasty infection of the lungs that had caused pneumonia. He became a regular visitor of hers. One day he approached the charge sister of that ward and asked if it were possible for them to be married in hospital.

They had both been widowed. The lady was a resident in a home for the elderly. The home changed her room from a single to a double. The man sold his home and moved in with his new bride.

I was fortunate to be on duty at the time the wedding took place. The man stood beside the bed of his new love. The lady, propped up on pillows, looked delicate and delightful in a lace night gown someone had bought for her. In the moment when he slipped the ring on her finger and kissed her, I realised that love knows no boundaries of age or time. Forty-one years later, I can still see the beautiful look of love on their faces as they said their vows… 'until death us do part.'

Now, when I doubt that a man would find me attractive, I remember that wonderful elderly couple. For whatever time they had together they were going to make the most of it, caring for and sharing with each other.

And doubts there have been. I have struggled with insecurities of my worthiness as a woman. How would a man react when he saw my aged body naked? Was I still capable of being sensual and sexually active? The comfort and security of being with someone who fully accepted me for who I was had gone. The thought of undressing for the first time in front of a man I hardly knew was rather frightening.

My Imagination

In my imagination my new lover,
handsome with stunning blue eyes, gazes
across a restaurant table into my soft brown eyes.
Should I be daring and return his gaze?
Does he want me to be
blatantly seductive or subtly sensual?
The lines on my face have been smoothed away
and my breasts returned to the youthful firmness
of forty years ago…….. in my imagination.
My fingers play with the wine glass stem.
His fingers (accidentally) brush against mine.
The thrill of that touch runs through my body.
In my imagination our feet slide against each other.
Our knees hint at touching. I worry about my perfume.
Would musk have been a better choice?
I notice his gaze has lowered to my throat,
then further down. I begin to blush.
Our knees make firmer contact.
My hair (no longer greying) spreads down my back,
a glory of auburn silk ……in my imagination.
I read the menu without glasses.
A long stemmed red rose lies parallel to my fork.
Beside the rose, a box of chocolates!
I am concerned. They may ruin my slim figure.
His voice, waves of the ocean, laps over my lustful sand.
I soak its tones into my depths. Beneath the surface
the undercurrent of words swirl with innuendoes.
The waitress collects our plates. Now there is open space.
No distractions, nowhere to hide. His hand no longer
plays at pretence; it slides over mine. Fingers entwine!
Were I to stand up I know my legs would tremble.
I know I would look a fool. I'd probably
stand on his toes or drop my bag on the floor.
In my imagination he has walked me to my door.

I pretend the night air chills me. He wraps me
in oh-so-warm arms. I melt into his embrace.
The first kiss is soft and dry. Then, within my mind's eye,
his mouth moves to my neck, then back across my face
to deliver a moist, passionate tongue-seeking kiss.
In my imagination I am not standing here washing dishes,
wondering what colour I will put in my greying hair, or
how I may lift my sagging breasts to a more youthful pose!

Again, through meditation, I came before my Master. I spoke of my fears to him. Softly, through the thought waves of my mind, he spoke.

"Why do you doubt? You have been told that the man who is coming to you will be your equal in all ways. When there is real love there is only love. All else falls away or falls into its rightful place. You will be loved and accepted for who you are in that moment. You already know real love begins within you. Seek, then, to be in that place of love. Your lover will not come until you are in that beautiful place of inner love. Your hunger to be loved is a cloud that covers the top of the mountain. It blocks your view. How can your lover see your beauty when you surround yourself with such a cloud? Your fears create an impenetrable wall between you and your lover. Let go of your fears. Let go of the need to be loved. Know that you are already loved. Know that you are love itself. Only then will he come to you."

There were those two magical words again... let go! How many times throughout my fifty-nine years have I blocked something coming to me by hanging on tightly to the fear that it may not happen? Here I was doing it again. In being hungry to feel a lovely man's arms around me, I was projecting the fear that it might not happen.

The ancient karmic law was being played out, what you give out is what you get back. In projecting my fear of never having a man to love me I was drawing to me that very situation.

The ancient law of attraction was where my focus needed to be. If I am at peace because I am in that place of inner love, and projecting that love in a natural way, then I would draw back to me the love of a beautiful man. I would see his inner beauty; he would see my inner beauty, and the magnetic force of that love and beauty would draw us together.

It seems to me that my whole life's journey is a singular lesson that can be summed up in two words... *let go!* Let go and trust the universal energy!

So be it!

Conclusion

In Meditation

In the depths of meditation you came to me, reached out and took my hands in yours. There was no voice, no need to utter unnecessary words.

Liquid love flowed from your being into mine, transforming me into a field of light, as you were. I laughed…silent, joyous laughter. Your lovely face, hugely smiling and full of fun, melted my heart.

I climbed back through the density of time to the leather chair where my body reclined; to the flickers of flames on red coals in the fire place.

Tears streamed down flushed cheeks, dripped onto my shirt, my body heavy with reality. But your presence filled the room, the essence of total tenderness!

I asked, "When do the tears stop?"

Through the silence of the night you answered, "When you let go of me and find love again."

અૐ

Since that meditation my new lover has come to me.

Both John and I have had to journey through the pain of grief. Three years before meeting me his wife died of cancer. For seven years and nine months I had to wait for him but the wait was worth every moment of longing for my new soul mate to step into my life.

Many times I doubted if I would ever find someone with whom I could share my journey. As the years slipped past the ability to 'let go' of the outcome of finding my new lover grew increasingly difficult. I began to wonder if I had imagined what Jeff had said to me…"There is another man coming into your life. Do not reject him. Do not turn away from him. He is coming to help you and you were destined to meet." Within the last six months before meeting John, my closest friends often heard me say, "Perhaps I am not meant to have a man in my life. Perhaps I am meant to journey alone."

Five men passed through my life; each one taught me what I did not want in my partner; each one showed me a quality I enjoyed. They were wonderful teachers who helped me to grow and expand as I waited for John.

Jeff was right…John and I have brought to each other a depth of healing and love that surpasses any that we have previously known. I did not think it possible that I could love more than I have done before, but I do. I believe the reason is that both John and I have done the hard work of moving through our grief as individuals, without the ability to rescue each other. We have both come into the knowledge of our own inner strengths; we have both cleaned up our own messes before stepping into new love.

John's and my past loves will remain forever beautiful memories in our minds, and each will hold a special place within our hearts…. after all it is these past loves that have helped to create who we are and helped us to prepare for each other. Love cannot die. John's love for those women who have played a major part in his awakening to self, and my love for the men who have done the same for me, will always remain in our hearts.

John and Joy wish to honour those past loves and to thank them for preparing us for each other.

It is my belief that Jeff and John's wife have worked together from the other side to bring us together. I see them smiling, I hear their joyful laughter.

My Darling

I am coming home to you,
to your body and your breath.
I have been too long away!
I ache to hear your voice,
its soft sensual undertones,
the intimate things you say.
I journeyed through dark forests
and the mountains of past lives.
I had to find my way.
But now I am coming home to you
through centuries of time
from a long forgotten day.
And I long to feel your hands
slide down my back again,
wandering where they may;
To gaze into your lovely eyes
and feel our souls reunite.
Yes, I have been too long away.
My Darling, I am coming home to you!

About the Author

As a young child, Joy became aware of her ability to see people in spirit form. Each time she tried to speak of her gift she was chastised for telling lies. Her experiences never faded but she learnt to keep them to herself.

In 2002 Joy's husband died of a heart attack whilst they were walking in the Australian bush close to their home. As she faced her future alone, she made up her mind to never hide her gift again.

Joy began using her abilities as a psychic medium (combined with her training in nursing, telephone counselling, Theta energy healing, and many other courses she has completed) to work in the field of grief healing. Her work has now expanded to include such issues as troubled relationships, depression, self awareness and self love, career changes, helping others to understand their psychic abilities and many other issues individuals struggle with throughout the course of their lives.

Joy has written poetry since 1973 and has had her poems published in anthologies and literary magazines in Australia, U.S.A, England and India. She has self published 3 volumes of poems and in 2003 launched her CD of poems backed with music. In 2004 Joy began the Reason-Brisbane Poetry Prize which has become Australia's most prestigious rural poetry competition. Some of Joy's poems can be seen on her web site www.joybrisbane.com

Lightning Source UK Ltd.
Milton Keynes UK
06 November 2010

162508UK00003B/4/P